ROUTE 66 NEW MEXICO

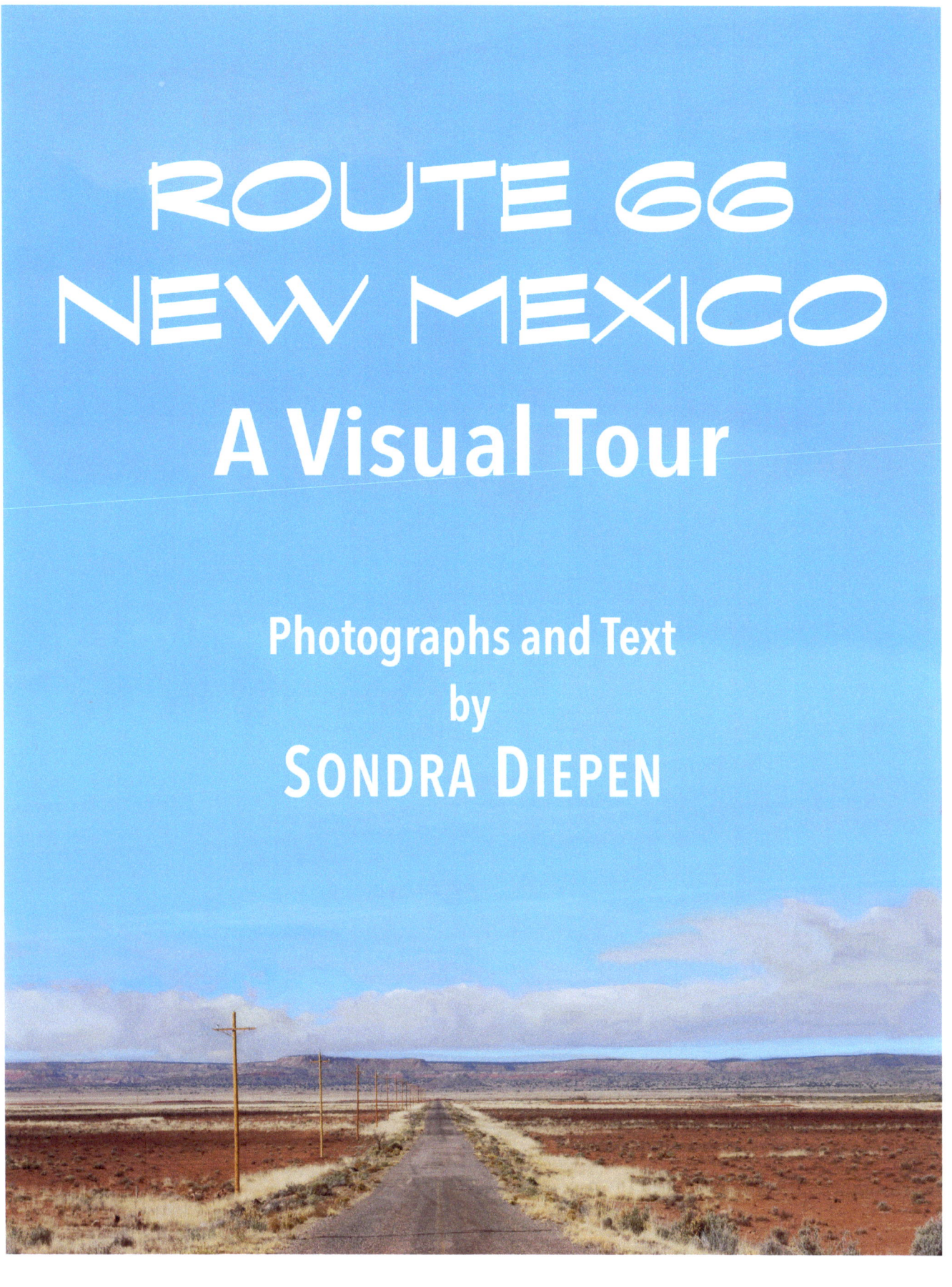

ROUTE 66 NEW MEXICO
A Visual Tour

Photographs and Text
by
SONDRA DIEPEN

© 2024 by Sondra Diepen
All Rights Reserved
No part of this book may be reproduced in any form or by any electronic or mechanical means including information storage and retrieval systems without permission in writing from the publisher, except by a reviewer who may quote brief passages in a review.

Sunstone books may be purchased for educational, business, or sales promotional use.
For information please write: Special Markets Department, Sunstone Press,
P.O. Box 2321, Santa Fe, New Mexico 87504-2321.
Printed on acid-free paper

Library of Congress Cataloging-in-Publication Data

Names: Diepen, Sondra, 1941- author.
Title: Route 66 New Mexico : a visual tour / photographs and text by
   Sondra Diepen.
Description: Santa Fe, NM : Sunstone Press, [2024] | Summary: "A
   photographic collection and guide with maps and histories of 51
   locations, sites, and attractions on Route 66 across New Mexico from the
   Texas border to the Arizona state line"-- Provided by publisher.
Identifiers: LCCN 2024031909 | ISBN 9781632934413 (paperback)
Subjects: LCSH: United States Highway 66--Guidebooks. | United States
   Highway 66--Description and travel. | United States Highway
   66--Pictorial works. | New Mexico--Guidebooks. | New Mexico--Description
   and travel. | LCGFT: Guidebooks.
Classification: LCC F794.3 .D54 2024 | DDC 917.89045--dc24/eng/20240728
LC record available at https://lccn.loc.gov/2024031909

Front cover image: *Looking North from Route 66 near Prewitt, New Mexico*.
   Photograph by Author.
Half title page image: *New Mexico Yucca (State Flower)*. Original drawing by
   Author, 2022.
Full title page image: *Route 66, Looking West from Correo, New Mexico*, 2014.
   Photograph by Author.
Back cover image: *Route 66 Survivor*, 2013. Photograph by Author.

Photo credits:
Carol L. Adamec: The Author and her sister in their dad's truck (page 5); the
   Author at the Route 66 Neon Drive-Thru in Grants, New Mexico (page 119);
   the Author and her dog, Zephyr (page 215).

Robert H. Diepen: Photograph of the Author, age 4 (page 214).

Photograph of the Author and friend taken by anonymous patron of Joseph's Bar
   & Grill (page 46).

Unless otherwise credited, all photographs were taken by the Author.

WWW.SUNSTONEPRESS.COM
SUNSTONE PRESS / POST OFFICE BOX 2321 / SANTA FE, NM 87504-2321 /USA
(505) 988-4418

DEDICATION

To my parents,
who took us on road trips to Yellowstone, to Glacier, to Yosemite,
and to The Gap Trading Post run by their friends, located in the heart
of the Navajo reservation in Arizona:
Thanks for the '63 Ford truck and the lust for travel.

To my sister Donna:
Thanks for coming along on my adventures.

Historic Route 66 sign

Contents

About This Book 13
Discovering Route 66 14–15
PART I: From the New Mexico–Texas Border to Santa Rosa

  Photograph 16
  Map 17
  GLENRIO, Exit 0 (Texas)
    Photographs 18–19
    Narrative: In Texas or New Mexico? 162
  ENDEE, Exit 369
    Photographs 20–21
    Narrative: From Rustlers to Rust 163
  SAN JON, Exit 356
    Photographs 22–23
    Narrative: Bypassed and Bygone Days 164
  CEDAR HILL, Exit 356
    Photographs 24–25
    Narrative: A Hilltop Rest Stop 164–165
  TUCUMCARI, Exits 335, 329
    Photographs 26–33
    Narrative: "Tucumcari Tonight!" 165
    Narrative: TePee Curios 165
    Narrative: The Historic Route 66 Motel 165–166
  MONTOYA, Exit 311
    Photographs 34–35
    Narrative: No More Mail 166
  NEWKIRK, Exit 300
    Photographs 36–37
    Narrative: Seen Better Days 166–167
    Narrative: The Goodnight-Loving Trail 167–168
  CUERVO, Exit 291
    Photographs 38–39
    Narrative: A Town Divided by Progress 168
  FRONTIER MUSEUM, Exit 284
    Photographs 40–41
    Narrative: A Wild West Attraction 168–169
  SANTA ROSA, Exits 277, 275, 273
    Photographs 42–47
    Narrative: "City of Natural Lakes" — in the Desert? 169–170

PART II: Route 66 Pre-1937: "The Santa Fe Loop"
From Santa Rosa to Los Ranchos de Albuquerque

- Narrative 48
- Map 49
- DILIA, US 84 & NM–119
  - Photographs 50–51
  - Narrative: First Stop on The Santa Fe Loop 172
- SAN JOSE, Exit 319 off I-25
  - Photographs 52–53
  - Narrative: Pecos River Crossing 172–173
- SANTA FE, Exits 284, 282B (North), 278 off I-25
  - Photographs 54–61
  - Narrative: The City Different 173-174
  - Narrative: Route 66 Vintage Motels 175
- SANTO DOMINGO, Exit 259 off I-25
  - Photographs 62–63
  - Narrative: "Where Real Indians Trade".................. 175–176
- ALGODONES, Exit 248 off I-25
  - Photographs 64–65
  - Narrative: Stone's Buffalo Trading Post, *aka* Rosa's Cantina 176–177
- BERNALILLO, Exit 240, off I-25
  - Photographs 66–67
  - Narrative: Silva's Saloon—A Family History 177
- LOS RANCHOS de ALBUQUERQUE, Exit 234 to 4th Street
  - Photographs 68–69

PART III: Route 66 Post-1937: "The Santa Fe Cut-Off"

- Narrative 70
- Map 71
- CLINES CORNER REST STOP, Exit 218 off I-40
  - Photographs 72–73
  - Narrative: Moving with the Road 180
- LONGHORN RANCH, Exit 203 off I-40
  - Photographs 74–75
  - Narrative: "Where the West Once Lived" 180–181
- THE HITCHING POST, Exit 196 off I-40
  - Photographs 76–77
  - Narrative: Snakes and Souvenirs 181

MORIARTY, Exits 197, 196, 194 off I-40
- Photographs 78–81
- Narrative: Home of the "Pinto Bean Fiesta" 182

MIDWAY TRADING POST, Exit 187 off I-40
- Photographs 82–83
- Narrative: A Restored Photo Op 183

EDGEWOOD, Exit 187 off I-40
- Photographs 84–85
- Narrative: Finding the Red Top Diner 183–184
- Narrative: About the Valentine Diners 184

ALBUQUERQUE, Exits 167, 158, 149 off I-40
- Photographs 86–97
- Narrative: The KiMo: An Iconic Theater 184–185
- Narrative: Maisel's Historic Indian Trading Post 185–186
- Narrative: The "City of Neon" on Route 66 186

PART IV: From Albuquerque to Milan

- Photograph 98
- Map 99

SUWANEE-CORREO, Exit 126 off I-40
- Photographs 100–101
- Narrative: Wild Times at the Wild Horse Mesa Bar 190

LAGUNA PUEBLO, Exit 114 off I-40
- Photographs 102–103

CASA BLANCA TRADING POST, Exit 104 off I-40
- Photograph 105

BUDVILLE, Exit 104 off I-40
- Photographs 106–107
- Narrative: Murder and Mayhem on Route 66 190–191

VILLA de CUBERO TRADING POST, Exit 104 off I-40
- Photographs 108–111
- Narrative: Fame, Fortune, and Pickles 191

MT. TAYLOR MOTEL, Exit 104 off I-40
- Photographs 112–113

SAN FIDEL, Exit 100 off I-40
- Photographs 114–115
- Narrative: "Welcome to Geezerville" 192

WHITING BROTHERS, Exit 96 off I-40
- Photographs 116–117
- Narrative: Gas for Less 193

GRANTS, Exits 85, 81 off I-40
- Photographs 118–121
- Narrative: "City of Spirit" 194

MILAN, Exits 81, 79 off I-40
- Photographs 122–125
- Narrative: Snakes and Snacks 194–195

PART V: From Milan to Beautiful Mountain Trading Post

Photograph 126
Map 127

BLUEWATER OUTPOST, Exit 72 off I-40
- Photographs 128–129
- Narrative: Curios Galore! 198
- Narrative: The Bluewater Motel 198

OLD CRATER TRADING POST, Exit 72 off I-40
- Photographs 130–131
- Narrative: Claude Bowlin, Friend of the Navajos 198–199

RATTLE SNAKE TRADING POST, Exit 72 off I-40
- Photographs 132–133
- Narrative: Dining, Dancing, and Snakes 199

PREWITT, Exit 63 off I-40
- Photographs 134–135
- Narrative: More Trading Post Histories 200

TOMAHAWK BAR, Exit 63 off I-40
- Photograph 137
- Narrative: A Reinvented Quonset Hut 200–201
- Narrative: About Quonset Huts 201

THOREAU, Exit 53 off I-40
- Photographs 138–139
- Narrative: From Rugs to Rubble 201

HERMAN'S GARAGE, Exit 53 off I-40
- Photographs 140–141
- Narrative: Gas and Repairs 202

BEAUTIFUL MOUNTAIN TRADING POST, Exit 53 off I-40
- Photographs 142–143

PART VI: From Beautiful Mountain Trading Post to the Arizona Border

    Photograph 144
    Map 145
    CONTINENTAL DIVIDE TOURIST STOP, Exit 47 off I-40
        Photographs 146–147
        Narrative: "Top o' the World" Tourist Stop 204–205
    GALLUP, Exits 26, 22, 20, 16, 12 off I-40
        Photographs 148–153
        Narrative: Gallup: The Heart of Red Rock Country 205
        Narrative: El Rancho Hotel 205–206
        Narrative: Ortega's Indian Jewelry Heaven 206–207
    CHIEF YELLOWHORSE TRADING POST, Exit 359 (Arizona) off I-40
        Photographs 154–155
        Narrative: "Make Chief Great Again" 207–208

Hasta Luego
    Photograph 157

The NARRATIVES: *Stories, Facts, and Tales* 159
    PART I 161–170
    PART II 171–177
    PART III 179–187
    PART IV 189–195
    PART V 197–202
    PART VI 203–208

Contributing Authors 209
Sources 209–210
If Not for Them 211
Final Words: Preservation of Route 66 212–213
About the Author 214–215

ABOUT THIS BOOK

Want to explore New Mexico's Route 66?

This book takes you on an in-depth, visual tour across the Land of Enchantment—from the Texas border to the Arizona state line.

For those who remember cruising Route 66 in their younger days; for those hoping one day to take a trip down Route 66; and for those travelers driving the Route—this book is for you!

Unlike many Route 66 guidebooks that feature just a few points of interest along New Mexico's portion of the Mother Road, this publication is a guide to 51 different locations, sites, and attractions across the state.

This book features 222 photographs I have taken over the past ten years along Route 66. The selected images reflect my creative perspective and response as a professional photographer to what I found interesting, curious, humorous, mysterious, and surprising.

The exit locations and simple site maps will assist the adventurous traveler in locating the Route 66 places I discovered.

Information, stories, conversations, and personal recollections became the narratives about most of the locations, sites, and attractions that appear in the photographs.

Whether reading about or visiting these places—with a little imagination, you can picture cattle rustlers, Pueblo dancers, vintage cafes, curio shops, and, of course, writhing snakes in concrete pits that once coaxed travelers to experience New Mexico's Route 66.

I invite you to meander along Route 66's designated stretches and now abandoned roadways that I traveled. There are others, too, and plenty of opportunities for photo ops, discoveries, and your own adventures while traveling east to west across New Mexico.

With this book, both road warriors and armchair travelers can tour the remnants of Route 66's past and visit the thriving enterprises still luring tourists, sightseers, and worldwide fans to the Mother Road in New Mexico.

Let your adventure begin.

Bowlin's Old Crater Trading Post near Bluewater, New Mexico, now closed. August 2012

Discovering Route 66

"Pull over. I've gotta see this! Look, there are paintings of Indians all along that wall."

While recording petroglyphs west of Albuquerque for the Bureau of Land Management, I spotted a deteriorating building partially hidden by bushes along a road paralleling I-40. Here it was! I had encountered Route 66 in New Mexico and this building was a relic of its colorful historic past.

Up until that moment, I had only been vaguely aware of Route 66, even though as a child I had traveled portions of it in California and Arizona with my parents. Seeing garish billboards featuring snakes, curios, and refreshments for travelers, I begged them to pull over. *Oh, no. Those are tourist traps. Not for us.* And we drove right by.

Ten years later on a road trip to New Mexico with my college friend Joanne, those same billboards tempted us to pull off the road. But those old parental warnings lingered in my memory. And we drove right by.

After moving to New Mexico in 1974, I began exploring back roads that were merely faint lines on a map. I've always been drawn to the broken down adobe house or a lonely recliner forsaken in the landscape. I once found someone's Army ring in the folds of a blue couch discarded on a hillside covered with sagebrush. How does a broken armchair or a rusted pickup bed end up there? Who were the owners? What were their dreams, and why did they give up and leave their possessions behind?

But I digress…The discovery that day of this dilapidated painted building known as Bowlin's Old Crater Trading Post sparked my fascination with Route 66. I especially sought out the road segments that had been cut off by better and straighter highways. In my quest for the remains of Route 66, I discovered structures, foundations, and broken glass. After awhile, I could recognize cement islands that had once served as gas pump anchors and building foundations of roadside rest stops. All of this provided a new focus for my photography.

Looking over hundreds of photographs taken over ten years, I realized I had the makings of a book…a visual tour of Route 66 across New Mexico. The sights and locations I had discovered spurred my interest in their histories. I began searching for information about these places. Traveling Route 66, back and forth from one border to the other to take yet one more photograph in a different light or in a different season, I met people who shared their stories and memories which formed the many narratives included in this book.

Since taking my first photograph of Bowlin's Old Crater Trading Post in 2012, these historic places have changed drastically: paintings are fading, walls are collapsing, neon signs are disappearing, and buildings are destroyed beneath the blade of a bulldozer. People have moved on and their villages have turned into ghost towns. And today's travelers, oblivious to the unique past of Route 66 in New Mexico, just drive right by.

In some ways this book is an anthropological and a historical record. Some places from this era are now just rubble or no longer exist. Yet, unlike Missouri, Oklahoma, and even Texas, we have a unique Western culture here that captivated travelers passing through New Mexico then, and still does to this day.

My ultimate hope in seeking out and photographing many of these way stations is that organizations, philanthropists, and lovers of the Mother Road will step up to preserve and restore what remains of our rich past. Fortunately, there are such organizations, state-based and national, that are doing just that. I hope you will support their efforts.

Lastly, I hope this book entices readers to take an exit off the interstate, slow down, and enrich your experience of Old Route 66. Seek out the sites, enjoy the narratives, and awaken your imagination to what travel on the Mother Road use to be like.

There still are authentic Route 66 curio shops and trading posts loaded with fascinating novelties, Western wear and souvenirs, and fine Native American jewelry and rugs that you won't find anywhere else. Sample the local chile, both "red and green", at a vintage cafe; or try Indian fry bread being sold along the side of the road. And relax at a restored motel for a night of dreams about Route 66.

It's still a great road trip.

Welcome to New Mexico, May 2021

PART 1

From the New Mexico-Texas Border to Santa Rosa

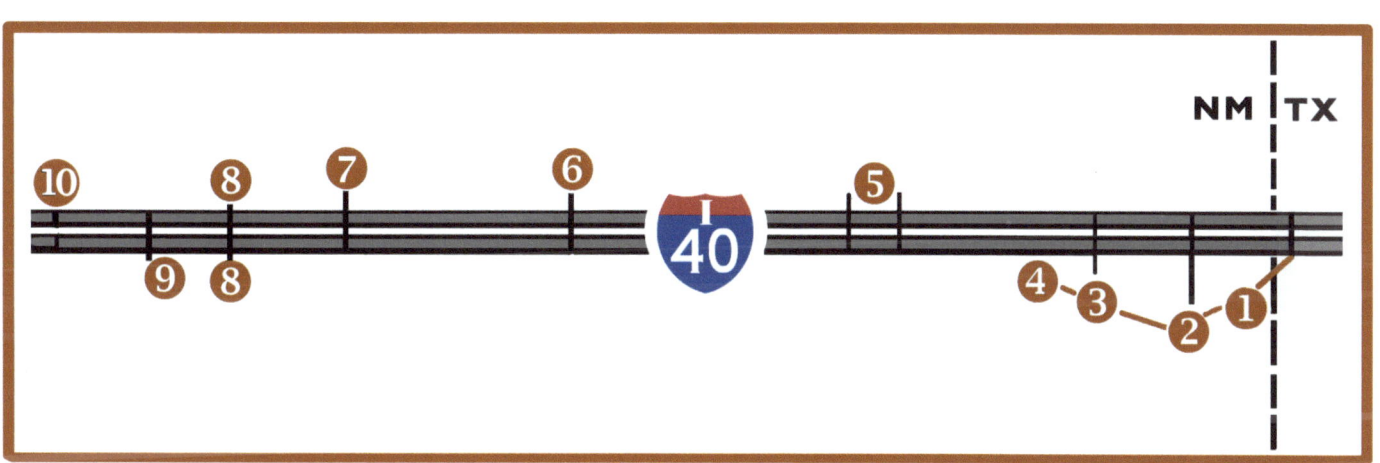

1. Glenrio, TX
2. Endee
3. San Jon
4. Cedar Hill
5. Tucumcari
6. Montoya
7. Newkirk
8. Cuervo
9. Frontier Museum
10. Santa Rosa

GLENRIO

Glenrio Garage, October 2019

Sombrero Diner, October 2019

Narrative on page 162

Glenrio Diner by the Road, August 2015

ENDEE

Endee, September 2013

Home in the Brush, 1950 Packard. November 2014

Narrative on page 163

Modern Rest Rooms, September 2013

SAN JON

Steve Gore Trading, September 2013

Western Motel, September 2013

San Jon Gas Pump, October 2019

CEDAR HILL

Cedar Hill Interior, November 2014

Back Door, September 2013

Narrative on page 164

Refuge for Radiators, October 2019

TUCUMCARI

Tucumcari Tonight! September 2020

Route 66 Survivor, September 2013

TUCUMCARI

Historic Route 66 Motel, June 2022

August 2021

Good Morning, Betty Boop, October 2019

TUCUMCARI

Mexican Foods, October 2019

Ken's Ice Cream Parlor (now closed).
September 2020

Narrative on page 165

Ranch House Cafe (now closed). October 2019

TUCUMCARI

Western Curios. Photo collage by Author and Carol L. Adamec, 2022

Narrative on page 165

TePee Curios, October 2013

MONTOYA

No More Mail, September 2013

No More Beer, September 2013

Narrative on page 166

Cool Cat, Cold Beer, September 2013

NEWKIRK

Overgrown Motel, August 2021

Vista Mini Mart Tanks, August 2021

Narrative on page 166

Wilkerson's, September 2020

37

CUERVO

Cuervo Post Office, Northside, October 2019

Route 66 Surplus, September 2013

Narrative on page 168

Cuervo Southside, Home Sweet Home, September 2013

Maytag, Retired, June 2018

1953 Ford, September 2013

FRONTIER MUSEUM

Cowboy Days 1, August 2021

Cowboy Days 2

Cowboy Days 3

Narrative on page 168

Frontier's Modern Mural, September 2013

SANTA ROSA

Pre-1937 Route 66 Sign, September 2020

This Way to Blue Hole, September 2020

RIP, Santa Rosa Cemetery, August 2021

Narrative on page 169

Old Santa Rosa de Lima Chapel, built in 1879. June 2022

SANTA ROSA

Wave to the Trucker, June 2022

Edsel, Discontinued, July 2020

Retired Seagrave, July 2017

Narrative on page 169

1930 Ford on a Stick, July 2020

SANTA ROSA

Sun 'n Sand, July 2020

A Couple of Chicks Drivin' 66 (The Author and friend), November 2017

Narrative on page 169

Sahara Lounge sign, now in Albuquerque awaiting restoration. July 2017

Route 66 Pre-1937: "The Santa Fe Loop"

Take US 84 north to travel the original Route 66 to Santa Fe and Albuquerque. September 2020

When Route 66 was first commissioned, if you wanted to reach Albuquerque traveling east to west, you turned right on to US 84 north out of Santa Rosa and headed towards Santa Fe. This scenic loop passed through several small Spanish land grant settlements—Dilia, Romeroville, Tecolote, Bernal, San Jose, Pecos, Glorieta, and Cañoncito—communities that prospered from the traffic the Route brought their way.

This 107 mile journey brought you to the historic Santa Fe Plaza where you could partake of the art scene, local history, native culture, and enjoy a grand stay at La Fonda Hotel.

Continuing the remaining 60 or so miles south to Albuquerque, however, required fortitude and steady nerves. About 15 miles out of Santa Fe, one had to negotiate La Bajada (The Descent), a steep 500-foot descent off an escarpment. Brake pads made of cloth smoked and burned as drivers attempted to slow their vehicles around the 26 switchbacks. Often passengers would disembark from vehicles, while the drivers negotiated the tricky turns. Going north from Albuquerque to Santa Fe tested gravity-fed carburetors, as cars had to drive in reverse up La Bajada's steep incline and around the tight U-turns. The road was treacherous and accidents were frequent.

If you survived the descent, the road would take you to Santo Domingo Trading Post on the Kewa Pueblo, and then on to Algodones, Bernalillo, Los Ranchos de Albuquerque, and into Albuquerque.

Eventually "The Santa Fe Cut Off"—the direct route between Santa Rosa and Albuquerque completed in January 1927—eliminated the daunting La Bajada.

Today cars speed 75 miles an hour up and down I-25 between Albuquerque and Santa Fe, barely noticing the scars of the original, snaking La Bajada Hill road.

Essay by Dorothy E. Noe

PART II

Route 66 Pre-1937:
"The Santa Fe Loop"
From Santa Rosa to Los Ranchos de Albuquerque

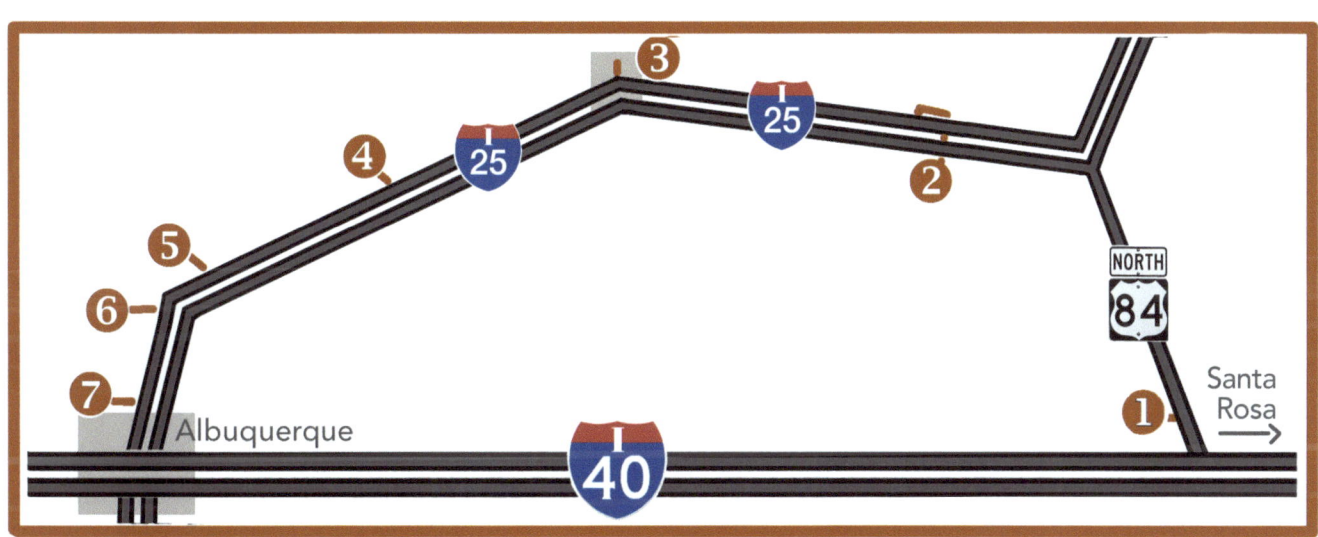

1. Dilia
2. San Jose
3. Santa Fe
4. Santo Domingo
5. Algodones
6. Bernalillo
7. Los Ranchos de Albuquerque

DILIA

Liquors and Wines, July 2020

Crumbling Wall, July 2020

Narrative on page 172

Sagrado Corazon Iglesia, built in 1900. July 2020

SAN JOSE

Route 66 Bridge over the Pecos, September 2020

Narrative on page 172

San Jose historic church, entrance. September 2020

San Jose historic church, back view. January 2015

SANTA FE
The City Different: A Historical Landmark

La Fonda, A Night's Stay Since 1607, September 2020

La Plazuela Restaurant at La Fonda. September 2020

SANTA FE
The City Different: Celebrating New Mexico's Arts

Dia de los Muertos Folk Art, September 2020

The New Mexico Museum of Art on the Santa Fe Plaza. September 2020

Images at left:
Bronze plaques, embedded in the sidewalk in front of
the New Mexico Museum of Art in Santa Fe, honor
more than eighteen artists—painters, sculptors, potters,
and writers—associated with New Mexico. January 2022

SANTA FE

The City Different: Unusual Sights

End of the Trail in Santa Fe, July 2019

Polar Bear, made of recycled car hoods. July 2019

SANTA FE
Route 66 Vintage Motel

July 2019

Narrative on page 175

July 2019

July 2019

July 2019

61

SANTO DOMINGO

Santo Domingo Trading Post, after the fire in 2001. January 2009

Santo Domingo Trading Post, restored in 2016. September 2021

Narrative on page 175

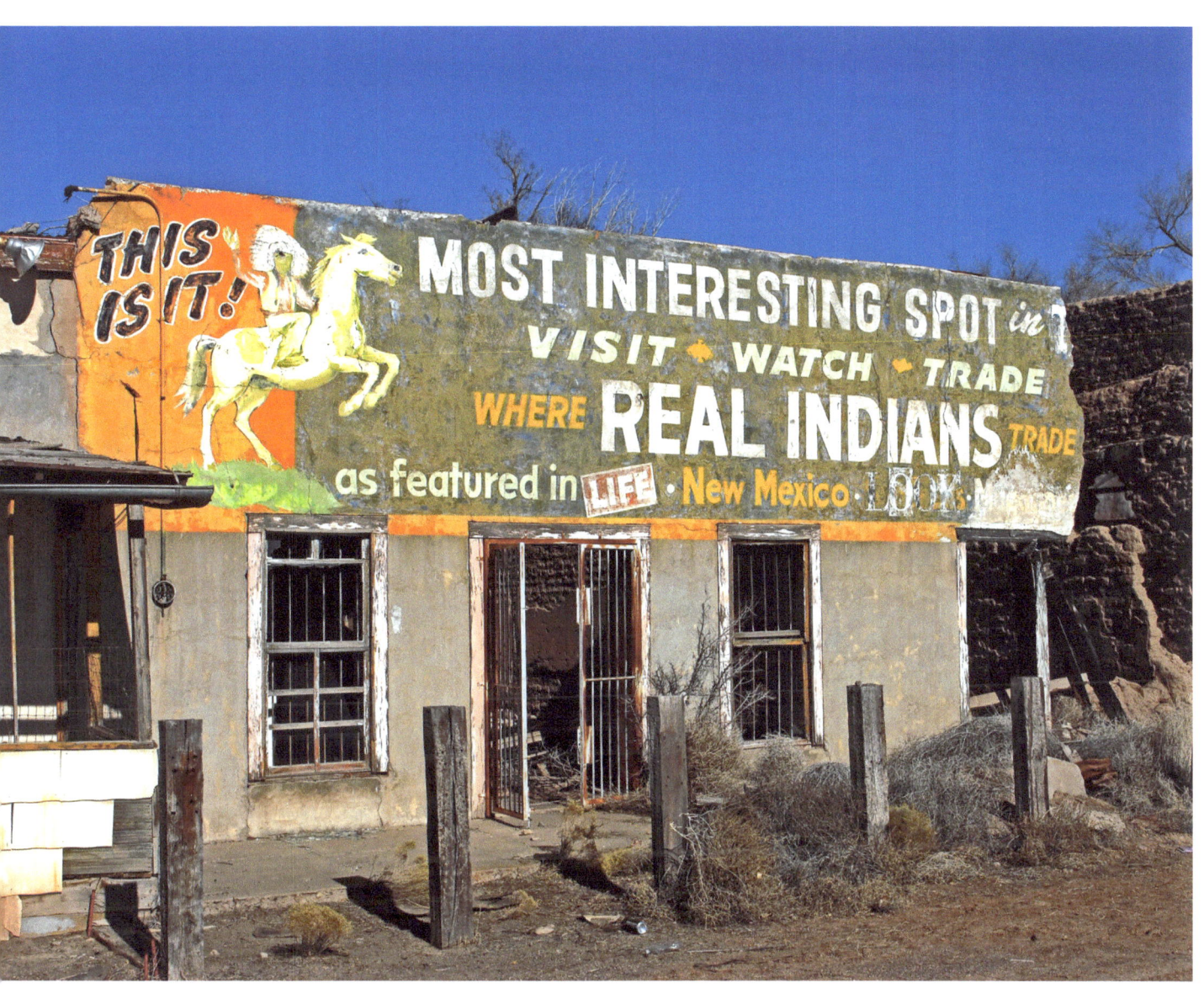

This Is It! Santo Domingo Trading Post. January 2009

ALGODONES

Stone's Buffalo Trading Post, aka Rosa's Cantina (before restoration). March 2020

New rug painting. June 2022

Old rug painting. September 2020

Narrative on page 176

Stone's Buffalo Trading Post, aka Rosa's Cantina (restored). July 2022

Old rug painting. September 2020

New rug painting. June 2022

65

BERNALILLO

Reserved Parking Now, December 2021

Reserved Parking Then.
Photograph of newspaper clipping (circa 1935) tacked to wall in Silva's Saloon. December 2021

Narrative on page 177

Range Cafe, Early Morning, June 2020

Los RANCHOS de ALBUQUERQUE

Motel on El Camino Real (4th Street NW), July 2020

El Camino Motor Hotel, built in the 1930s on the Santa Fe Loop, is still in operation. September 2021

Route 66 Post-1937: "The Santa Fe Cut-Off"

The commercial benefits to the small towns along Route 66's Santa Fe Loop between Santa Rosa and Santa Fe were short-lived. These small hamlets were soon to be the victims of political turmoil in the State's capital.

1926 was an election year and the campaign for the New Mexico governorship between the incumbent, Governor Hannett, and his opponent Richard Dillon, was bitter and divisive. After losing his bid for re-election, Governor Hannett— a Democrat—drew a straight line from Santa Rosa directly west to Moriarty (which was already connected to Albuquerque). He then ordered the New Mexico Highway Department to build a new 69-mile roadway between the two towns—thereby bypassing Route 66 to Santa Fe and punishing his Republican rivals and the next governor in Santa Fe. The only catch? There were only 31 days left in Hannett's term ending on January 1, 1927, to accomplish this engineering feat.

With the support of the workers in the Highway Department, two crews worked through Christmas Day— one working from Santa Rosa and the other from Moriarty, intent on meeting up at Palma, New Mexico. They marshaled a ragtag collection of equipment and, despite snow, wind, and bitter cold, felled thick forests and cut through private fences to meet the deadline.

After his swearing in on January 1, Governor Dillon dispatched an engineer to check out just what was going on in Palma. The fellow discovered cars traveling on a newly graded gravel road that connected Santa Rosa directly to Albuquerque, reducing Route 66 travel in New Mexico by 107 miles. The local folks called the new road segment "Hannett's Revenge." Others named it "Hannett's Joke."

By 1937 "The Santa Fe Cut-Off" was paved and officially became U.S. Route 66 between Santa Rosa and Albuquerque. As a result, Albuquerque's population more than tripled between 1937 and 1950. Santa Fe's attitude? Only a shrug.

This Way to Albuquerque, September 2020

Santa Fe remained the unique "City Different," attracting eager tourists as it still does today, with its unique adobe architecture and an exotic blend of art, culture, archaeology, and history.

Meanwhile, all along this new segment of Route 66, the growing number of motorists gave rise to mom-and-pop businesses, gas stations and repair garages, rest stops, diners, motor courts, curio shops, along with creative and outlandish roadside attractions to tempt tourists to stop at their establishments.

Essay by Dorothy E. Noe

PART III

Route 66 Post-1937:
"The Santa Fe Cut-Off" From Santa Rosa to Albuquerque

① Clines Corners
② Longhorn Ranch
③ The Hitching Post
④ Moriarty
⑤ Midway Trading Post
⑥ Edgewood
⑦ Albuquerque

CLINES CORNERS

July 2020

Clines Corners Rest Stop, July 2020

Narrative on page 180

Watching for Travelers, Clines Corners entryway. June 2022

LONGHORN RANCH

Sorry, No Vacancy, June 2022

Longhorn Ranch, August 2015

The HITCHING POST

Snakes and Souvenirs, closed in 1967. September 2013

Wall paintings. May 2013

Wall paintings. May 2013

Make a Wish, November 2014

MORIARTY

Under New Management...Again! June 2015 / November 2020

Narrative on page 182

1946 Dodge Ram, April 2015

MORIARTY

Rusting Relics, Lewis's Auto & Toy Museum. Photo collage by Author and Carol L. Adamec, 2022

Narrative on page 182

We Fix Flats, November 2014

MIDWAY TRADING POST

RV Park Watertower, east of Edgewood. May 2013

Narrative on page 183

Midway Trading Post—Before, May 2013

Midway Trading Post—Now, November 2014

83

EDGEWOOD

Red Top Diner Interior I, August 2020

Red Top Diner Interior II, August 2020

Narrative on page 183

Out to Lunch, May 2013

ALBUQUERQUE

KiMo Theatre Neon, November 2020

Narrative on page 184

KiMo Theatre, built in 1927 on Route 66 (Central Avenue). November 2014

ALBUQUERQUE

Public Art at Albuquerque's International Airport.
October 2020

Alvarado Transportation Center, downtown Albuquerque. October 2020

ALBUQUERQUE

Route 66 Diner, built in the Streamline Style of the 1940s. October 2020

Signs of the Times, at the Route 66 Diner. October 2020

Narrative on page 185

Historic Maisel's Indian Trading Post entry, with Indian head neon sign. November 2014

ALBUQUERQUE

The Lumberjack Disarmed, July 2016

The Lumberjack Rearmed, August 2020

Holy Cow! What a View, July 2016

ALBUQUERQUE
City of Neon

Westward Ho, March 2017

Desert Sands, July 2016

Piñon Motel, July 2016

Narrative on page 186

El Vado Neon, Restored, November 2018

ALBUQUERQUE

Zia Motor Lodge, March 2017

La Puerta Lodge, March 2017

El Don Motel, July 2016

Los Alamitos Motel Vintage Sign, October 2018

PART IV

From Albuquerque to Milan

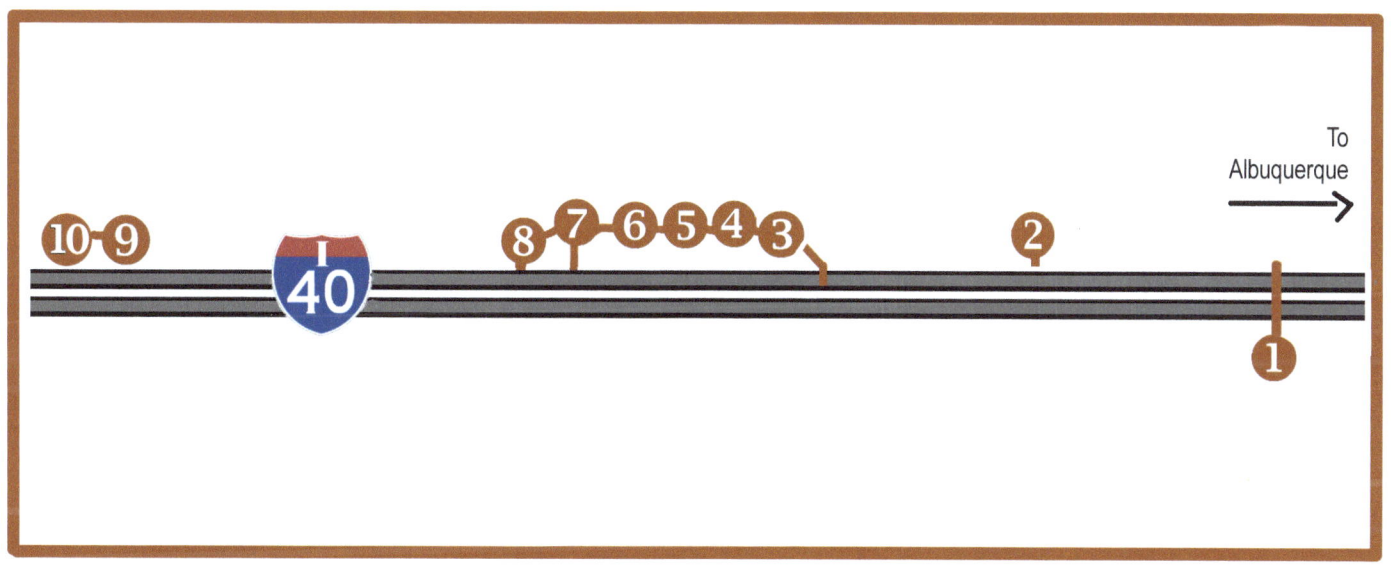

1. Suwanee-Correo
2. Laguna Pueblo
3. Casa Blanca Trading Post
4. Budville
5. Villa de Cubero
6. Mt. Taylor Motel
7. San Fidel
8. Whiting Brothers
9. Grants
10. Milan

SUWANEE - CORREO

Wild Times at Wild Horse Mesa Bar, Suwanee. March 2013

Narrative on page 190

Dark Sky, Correo. September 2013

Post Office & Trading Post, Correo. August 2014

LAGUNA PUEBLO

Roadside Curio Booth, Bypassed, January 2013

Fry Bread and Curios, August 2020

CASA BLANCA TRADING POST

Casa Blanca Caddy, April 2019

BUDVILLE

I-40 Traffic Bypassing Budville, July 2014

Bud's Cabins and Truck, June 2014

Narrative on page 190

Budville Murders, Scene of the Crime, June 2014

VILLA de CUBERO

The original Cubero Trading Company, circa 1930s. Photograph used with permission from Keith Gottlieb.

The original Cubero Trading Company today. June 2021

Narrative on page 191

Villa de Cubero Trading Post on Route 66's 1937 alignment.
Photograph used with permission from Keith Gottlieb.

VILLA de CUBERO

Narrative on page 191

Villa de Cubero Trading Post today on Historic Route 66. August 2020

Looking for Hemingway, April 2014

111

MT. TAYLOR MOTEL

April 2012

Seen Better Days, November 2012

Twisted Sign, April 2012. Mt. Taylor Motel dates back to 1945-1950.

SAN FIDEL

Do Not Enter,
April 2019

Welcome to Geezerville, September 2020

Acoma Curio Shop,
April 2019

Narrative on page 192

Old Shop in San Fidel, June 2019

WHITING BROTHERS

No Protecto, July 2014

Glass Station, January 2017

Narrative on page 193

Whiting Brothers at Sunset, January 2017

GRANTS

The Native Basket Array Public Art Project

Design by Gilbert Waconda, Laguna Pueblo. July 2020

Design by Sam Chavez, Acoma Pueblo. July 2020

Design by Ernest Skeet, Navajo Nation. July 2022

Narrative on page 194

Author at Route 66 Neon Drive-Thru.

GRANTS

Canton Cafe sign. September 2019

Hollywood Diner sign. October 2018

The West Theatre sign. September 2019

Narrative on page 194

Sands Motel 1/2 Block West, September 2019

Cobra Garden Palms, August 2018

Narrative on page 194

Cobra Gardens Mural, June 2012

Buy Sell Trade, Kachina Country USA store. 2016–2020

WOW Diner Reflections, August 2012

Not for Sale, Bluewater Motel sign. July 2022

PART V

From Milan to Beautiful Mountain T.P.

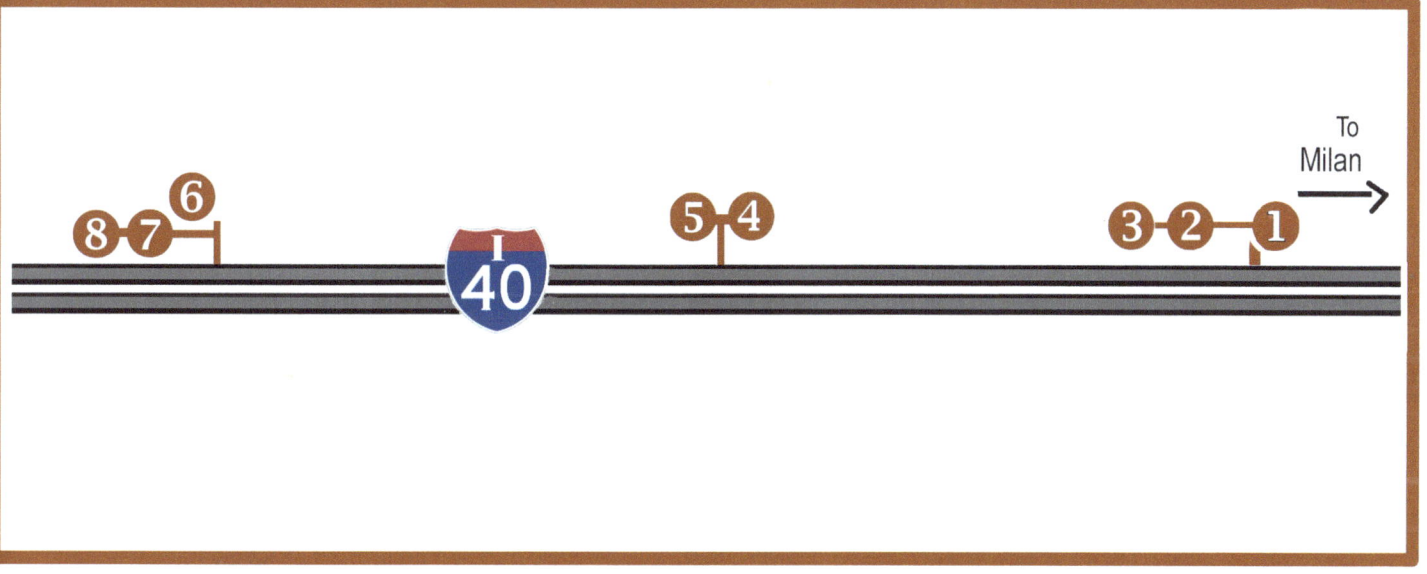

1. Bluewater Outpost
2. Old Crater Trading Post
3. Rattle Snake Trading Post
4. Prewitt
5. Tomahawk Bar
6. Thoreau
7. Herman's Garage
8. Beautiful Mountain Trading Post

BLUEWATER OUTPOST

Narrative on page 198

Get Ready to Fill Your Suitcase! Photo collage by Author and Carol L. Adamec, 2022.

OLD CRATER TRADING POST

Old Crater Trading Post Murals (below and continued on next page). August 2012–August 2018.

Narrative on page 198

Old Crater Trading Post, July 2020

RATTLE SNAKE TRADING POST

Reappearing Snake Mural, August 2018

Narrative on page 199

Rattle Snake Trading Post, August 2014

133

PREWITT

Zuni Mountain Trading Post, July 2020

Narrative on page 200

Hello? Hello? August 2012

TOMAHAWK BAR

Narrative on page 200

Package Liquor Only, August 2013

THOREAU

Navajo Rugs and Jewelry (side view), November 2012

Navajo Rugs and Jewelry (final view), April 2019

Narrative on page 201

Navajo Rugs and Jewelry (front view), November 2012.
Collection of the Bernalillo County 1% for Public Art Program, Albuquerque, New Mexico

HERMAN'S GARAGE

Herman's Gas Pump, July 2020

Herman's Dog, September 2019

Herman's 1940 Plymouth, August 2012

BEAUTIFUL MOUNTAIN TRADING POST

Herds Ahead, September 2020

Beautiful Mountain Mural, attributed to Richard Jim, Navajo artist. August 2012

Cattle, horses, sheep, wool, mohair, and piñon were sold here. August 2012

Bogie and Marilyn Billboard, July 2022

PART VI

From Beautiful Mt. to the Arizona Border

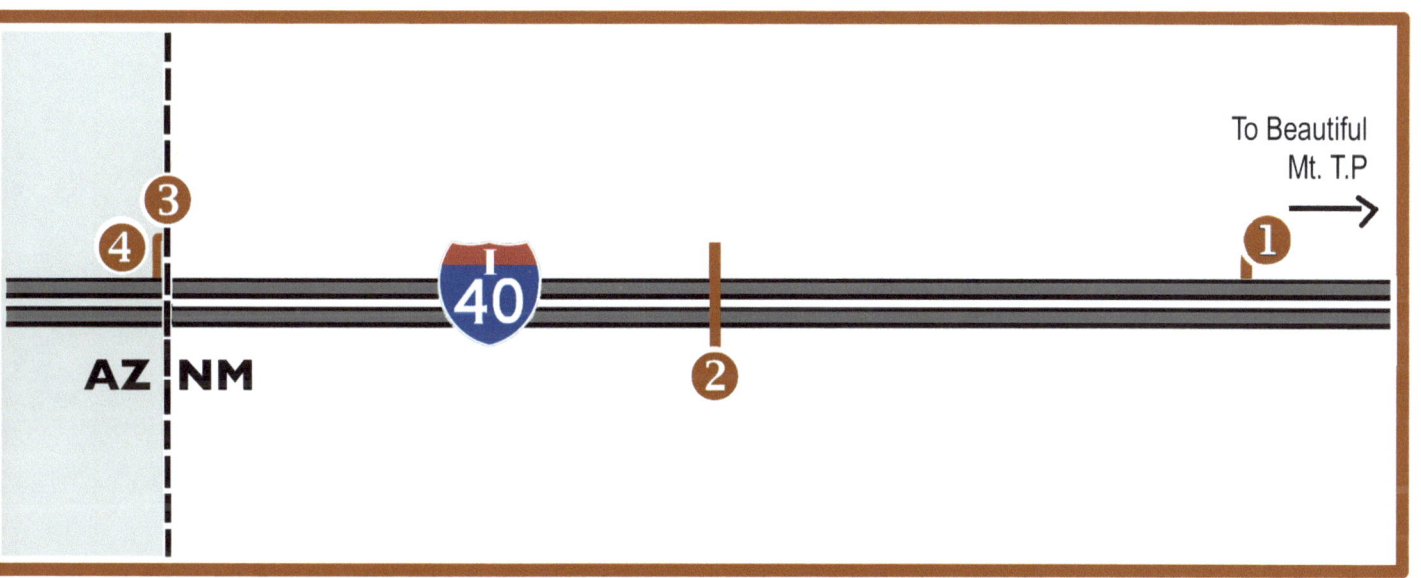

1. Continental Divide Tourist Stop
2. Gallup
3. Chief Yellowhorse Cave
4. Chief Yellowhorse Trading Post (AZ)

CONTINENTAL DIVIDE TOURIST STOP

Jewelry Straight Ahead, March 2014

Narrative on page 204

Top of the World Shopping, September 2020

Replicas, March 2014

147

GALLUP

Gallup's Neon Row. All photos: September 2019

Narrative on page 205

A Night Among the Stars, September 2019

GALLUP

Still Trading with Native Americans since 1913, September 2020

Sentinels, September 2020

Narrative on page 205

Turquoise, Rugs, and Saddles, August 2013

151

GALLUP

Kachina Grande, August 2020

Narrative on page 206

On Route 66 in Gallup is one of Ortega's many jewelry outlets in the Southwest. September 2020

153

CHIEF YELLOWHORSE TRADING POST

The original Chief Yellowhorse business at Cave of the Seven Devils, on the New Mexico-Arizona state line. July 2022

Chief Yellowhorse Says..., August 2020

154

Yellowhorse Travel Center, just over the New Mexico state line in Lupton, Arizona. August 2020

Hasta Luego

New Mexico Sunset, January 2013

The NARRATIVES

Stories, Facts, and Tales

PART I
Narratives

FROM THE NEW MEXICO-TEXAS BORDER TO SANTA ROSA

Glenrio
Endee
San Jon
Cedar Hill
Tucumcari
Montoya
Newkirk
Cuervo
Frontier Museum
Santa Rosa

Glenrio

Exit 0 (Texas) off I-40

In Texas or New Mexico?

With the new century a mere five years old, a few intrepid folks settled down establishing a new outpost in the American Southwest. In 1905 nobody seemed to care that half the town of Glenrio would be in west Texas and the other half in east New Mexico.

A year later a train station was built on the Texas side. When the post office was constructed, it lay on the west side of town—in New Mexico. Straddling the state line caused a rash of problems. For one, mail arrived at the train station in Texas and had to be transported to the post office in New Mexico. Not a big problem you may think; but if you wanted to wet your whistle, consider this. Because of Blue Laws, the Texas side was a dry county named Deaf Smith. New Mexico, on the other hand, had no problem serving alcohol. By 1920 a profusion of bars and dance halls had sprouted up on the New Mexico side. However, if you needed gas, all the stations were built on the Texas side where the gasoline tax was considerably less costly.

Ultimately Glenrio grew to have motels, a hardware store, grocery stores, cafes, and a newspaper, *The Glenrio Tribune*. After Route 66 was completed in 1926, Glenrio, midway between Amarillo and Tucumcari, prevailed by catering to weary travelers stopping for food, supplies, and oftentimes a night's rest.

In 1952 the Little Juarez Cafe opened, most likely designed to resemble the portable Valentine diners. Instead it was a stationary building constructed of concrete block. It operated until 1975 when the new I-40 bypassed Glenrio, marking the demise of the community.

Glenrio also has a few Hollywood claims to fame. Shortly after Route 66 was paved in 1937, a movie crew spent three weeks here filming part of *The Grapes of Wrath*. More recently, Pixar came here to get ideas for the animated film *Cars*.

If you visit Glenrio, facing east, look for what's left of the motel sign that used to say, "Motel: First Stop in Texas." If you were headed west, it said, "Motel: Last Stop in Texas." Even though Glenrio has become a ghost town, it is still a favorite photo op location for Route 66 enthusiasts.

Endee

Exit 369 off I-40, south on NM-93

From Rustlers to Rust

Endee, named for the cattle brand ND of a local ranch, was founded in 1882. By 1886 a post office was established which operated until 1955.

Endee was quite the Wild West town during its heyday. Cowboys from the area whooped it up on weekends with liquor and guns. Rumor has it that behind the saloon a ditch was dug each week to bury Saturday night's casualties.

Early in the 1900s the ranchers of eastern New Mexico Territory were losing cattle to a band of rustlers. Eventually the New Mexico Mounted Police stepped in. They spent over a month chasing the thieves throughout the region to no avail. They finally came up with a plan to hang out in Endee in hopes the outlaws would come to town to quench their thirst. After a long wait, the gang's ring leaders, John Fife and Tom Darlington, rode into town. The Mounted Police, hidden from view, leaped out and captured them on May 2, 1906. This marked the beginning of the end of cattle rustling in the territory.

Route 66 ran through Endee up until 1952 when the road was rerouted to the north. Before this new alignment, a motel had been built consisting of three rooms, each with its own garage and "Modern Restrooms."

Across the street is an extensive graveyard of old wrecked cars dating back to the 1940s and '50s. They now rest among the brush and mesquite, surrounded by a sturdy barbed wire fence. An easy to read "No Trespassing" sign is hung every twenty yards.

Nowadays, taking the Endee exit 369 off of I-40 and heading north will lead you to Russell's Truck and Travel Center. The 24-hour Center features a free museum of restored vintage cars, a sit down restaurant, food-to-go, gas, showers, and Route 66 souvenirs galore.

If you turn south you can travel down the two-lane road #93 to the original town of Endee. The old motel is overgrown, but the "Modern Restrooms" still stand.

Modern Rest Rooms, Endee, New Mexico

San Jon

Exit 356 off I-40

Bypassed and Bygone Days

The installation of railroads in the late 1800s and early 1900s changed the landscape of New Mexico. With access to trains, ranchers running sheep and cattle on large expanses of land were now able to get supplies faster and move their animals to market without driving them hundreds of miles across the prairie. Towns along the tracks sprung to life to handle mail, merchandise, and meat. In 1902 San Jon was the first of these railroad settlements west of the Texas border and soon became a bustling community.

Twenty-four years later, in 1926, surveyors charted Route 66's path through San Jon, in time for Americans to hit the road in their Model Ts and Model As that were rapidly rolling off Ford assembly lines. Folks arrived in San Jon needing fuel and accommodations, and San Jon was happy to provide gas stations, motels, cafes, and diners.

In 1981 the new I-40 bypassed San Jon to the north. Less traffic drove through town and the tourist trade dwindled. Businesses closed and owners left for jobs elsewhere.

A small community still remains in San Jon, including a town park, a baseball field, at least one operating motel, and a restaurant. Today as you drive down Old Route 66, mostly shells of gas stations remain in the once lively village standing in silent testimony to better days.

Cedar Hill

8 Miles West of San Jon on Route 66

A Hilltop Rest Stop

Cedar Hill was once an active stop for travelers and locals alike. The few abandoned buildings still standing once offered gas, groceries, and a night's rest. Today the crumbling remains are located at the top of a steep hill.

Back in the day of inadequate automobile cooling systems and scarce places to obtain water, many radiators would boil over while attempting to travel east up this steep incline. When the travelers reached the top, they would pull over at the station asking for water to cool off their engines and to refill their Desert Bags—if they had one. They probably bought a cold soda pop at the store for themselves and their stressed out families as well.

This section of Route 66 between Santa Rosa and Amarillo, Texas, was only two narrow lanes and quite dangerous. People referred to it with grim humor as Death Alley. Later, when Route 66 was upgraded, this two-lane stretch was the last to be widened. Many of those old wrecked cars near Endee are likely the casualties of that narrow, two-lane highway. Those vehicles now lay rusting in their graveyard of brush and mesquite trees that have grown up over the years of abandonment.

Gas pump anchor pad

Like Endee, only the ghosts of Route 66 travelers wander Cedar Hill these days. Everyone has gone away, the gas pumps have disappeared, but a ragged recliner still remains.

Tucumcari
Exits 335, 329 off I-40 onto Route 66

"Tucumcari Tonight!"

Many communities between the Texas border and Santa Rosa, New Mexico, are the result of railroad tracks pushing westward. When the Chicago, Rock Island and Pacific line arrived at this spot in 1901, the company established a workers camp; and people started calling it Ragtown. As was often the case, saloons, dance halls, gambling joints, and outlaws moved right in. Thanks to this wild and brawling crowd, "Six-Shooter Siding" became the town's new nickname. By 1908 things had settled down, and *tucumcari*—a Comanche word meaning "Lookout"—was chosen as the town's final name.

In the early 1900s, after government land in Oklahoma had been snapped up by settlers, land around Tucumcari was still readily available to homesteaders. Thanks to continued railroad expansion delivering supplies and services, the town began to grow.

When Route 66 ran through the town in 1926, Tucumcari prospered. It took a downward turn when the Great Depression hit in the 1930s, followed by the Dustbowl. By 1940 the drought and Depression had ended, and increasing numbers of people began traveling again. As fortune would have it, businesses not only came back but expanded to accommodate the new tourist trade.

Although Tucumcari was adversely effected in the 1970s by the I-40 bypass, the town has retained its Old Route 66 feel to this day. There are still many remodeled motor courts, motels, and restaurants to visit, along with plenty of souvenirs to take home.

TePee Curios

TePee Curios is a must stop. As a building it has had a long and curious life. In 1944 Leland Hayes ran it as a Gulf Station, auto shop, and grocery, with a few souvenirs thrown in for good measure. When Route 66 was widened in 1959, the gas pumps had to be removed, creating space for the teepee-shaped entrance to be built.

Under new owners, the famous neon sign was added in 1960. Time, however, took its toll and the sign languished. In 2003, supported with federal funds from the New Mexico Route 66 Neon Sign Restoration Project, the TePee Curio's sign was refurbished and now brightens the evening sky.

The Historic Route 66 Motel

The Historic Route 66 Motel is a convenient place to rest for the night—especially if you have a dog. Next door is a large city park where you can take your pooch for an early morning walk—in your PJs if you like.

The motel, built in 1963, was originally named Royal Palacio designed in the International Style. This modern design was very popular in Palm Springs, California, in the early 1950s. Referred to as "Palm Springs Modern" this style was adapted for the desert environment, featuring rectangles of glass and steel and devoid of decoration.

The motel's name was changed around 2005 and the accommodations were restored to their original state. Only a few electrical changes were necessary.

The new owner, a former Naval air traffic controller, loved post-WWII aircraft. Coming across slightly crashed, banged-up Cessna 120s for sale, he quickly plunked down cash for two of them. The aircraft were trucked from Barstow, California, to Tucumcari and are now on display, attracting lodgers to spend the night at the Historic Route 66 Motel.

Montoya

Exit 311 off I-40

No More Mail

In the community of Rountree, the first post office opened in 1901. Henry Rountree became its first postmaster. The very next year, the town was renamed Montoya, and the Chicago, Rock Island & Pacific railroad arrived.

The railroad company chose Montoya to house its work crews as they continued laying tracks westward. The town quickly became the loading point for needed incoming supplies and sending cattle to the Chicago stockyards. Montoya grew to sport a hotel, a bank, several bars, and a dance hall.

In 1908 G. W. Richardson built his general store. He supplied ranchers, railroad workers, and the community with needed items like buckets, feed, groceries, saddle blankets, and windmill parts. Eventually, the post office was moved into his new establishment and the store became the town's gathering place.

In 1918 the dirt road from Tucumcari west to Santa Rosa was upgraded, and the highway work crews were housed in Montoya. Richardson, recognizing an opportunity, moved his wooden store across the railroad tracks into a sandstone building to be closer to the newly graded road, soon to be designated as Route 66.

In 1937 the post office moved for the second time into his spacious building which again became the community hub. Of course, more automobiles and improved roads meant more people traveling Route 66. Richardson, ever the entrepreneur, wisely added a Sinclair gas station to his enterprise. His business prospered until 1970. The arrival of I-40 bypassing Route 66 and Montoya led to his business going into decline. Richardson hung on until the mid 1970s when he finally closed his doors for good. In 1978 Richardson's store was added to the National Register of Historic Places. Today, sadly, the store is basically in ruins.

And, the postman no longer stuffs US mail into the open boxes.

Newkirk

Exit 300 off I-40

Seen Better Days

Until the late 1800s, no one really even paused to stop by what is now the town of Newkirk. James Conant was first to start ranching in the area, and the surrounding settlement took on his name.

When the railroad tracks arrived in 1901, the town of Conant was officially on the map but was soon to be rechristened. In Scottish-English, *kirk* is a church and Newkirk means "new church." For reasons lost to history, the town of Conant became Newkirk.

By 1902 the railroad company had built a station and a siding for supplies and equipment being delivered to the town, making Newkirk the area's only distribution center. Fifty years later, when Conchas Dam was constructed 26 miles to the north, supplies and materials needed for this project were handled at the Newkirk siding. In reality it was the last hurrah for Newkirk.

By 1910 the post office opened for business. Wilkerson's Store and Gulf gas station opened in 1925—one year before Route 66's arrival created a minor business boom. By the mid-1930s Newkirk's population peaked at 240 before a gradual decline began.

By the 1940s only 115 residents called Newkirk home. It still boasted four gas stations, two cafes, several cabins for rent, DeBaca's Trading Post and, of course, Wilkerson's Store. However, in the mid-1970s when the new east-west I-40 interstate bypassed Newkirk, commerce basically came to a halt.

Surprisingly, under the direction of the Wilkerson children, the store managed to stay open another ten years or so until lack of business prompted the family to close up shop.

Today the building is a shattered hull. But if you look closely, the fading painted name "Wilkerson's" can still be read on the front wall under the canopy. As you glimpse inside there are a few remaining dust-coated items hanging on the wall and an open book with curled, yellowed pages giving the sense of a once well stocked general store.

The 2010 census for Newkirk listed seven residents. By 2013 everyone had moved on.

THE GOODNIGHT-LOVING TRAIL

Just west of Newkirk is the site of some Wild West history. Route 66 crosses the famed Goodnight-Loving cattle trail which was featured in the novel, movie, and television mini-series "Lonesome Dove." There are no markers on Old Route 66 indicating the thousands of cattle herded north through these wide open spaces. The vistas appear today much as they did during those post-Civil War days.

Sign for historic site posted on I-40 just east of Newkirk exit 300

This legendary trail began in the mid-1860s when Charles Goodnight, Oliver Loving, and eighteen cowpunchers drove 2,000 head of longhorn cattle from Texas to Fort Sumner. They hoped to sell them to the military to feed the 8,000 imprisoned Navajos at Bosque de Redondo where supplies were running low. The Fort, however, bought only some of the steers. Goodnight and Loving decided to drive the remainder of the herd north, where the cattle were sold to a rancher in Denver.

A year later while driving another herd out of Texas, Comanches attacked and Loving was severely wounded. He managed to return to Fort Sumner where his gangrenous arm was amputated. He died two weeks later in September 1867.

Charles Goodnight continued his cattle driving and later became a ranch manager for a 1.3 million acre property in Palo Duro Canyon, Texas, that grazed over 100,000 head of cattle. Eventually he acquired his own ranch and became famous for breeding buffalo-Angus cattle hybrids. Over the years he was instrumental in establishing business, civic, and philanthropic organizations in the Texas panhandle.

In 1929 Goodnight died at the age of ninety-three. He was honored in 1958 as one of the first inductees into the National Cowboy Hall of Fame in Oklahoma City.

Cuervo
Exit 291 off I-40

A Town Divided by Progress

Cuervo is Spanish for crow.

Between 1901 and 1903 the Chicago, Rock Island Gulf Railroad laid tracks from the Texas border to Moriarty, New Mexico, where they hooked up with other railroad lines heading southwest. The trains provided needed goods and materials, allowing communities to spring up alongside the railroad tracks.

A siding was built where trains stopped to take on water and this location became known as Cuervo. In 1910 land in the area was opened for cattle ranching, and Cuervo's existence provided ranchers the needed supplies for their new venture.

When Route 66 was built in 1926, travelers drove through these towns, frequently needing gasoline, motels, and restaurants. Cuervo's population grew over time and peaked with 300 residents in the 1930s. The town boasted two schools, two churches, two motor courts and, more importantly, two doctors. By 1945, however, the population had dwindled by half as travel decreased due to tire and gasoline rationing during the Second World War.

The worst blow to the community came in the early 1970s with the arrival of I-40. The four-lane highway cut Cuervo in two and interstate traffic roared through at 75 miles an hour. Homes were left on the south side of I-40 and businesses on the north side.

Today many of the houses still stand, although numerous ones are abandoned and deteriorating. A few intrepid souls still make Cuervo their home.

Frontier Museum
Exit 284 off I-40

J. B. Stetson designed the first Western-style cowboy hat in 1865.

A Wild West Attraction

William and Lucy Wilson hailed from Texline, Texas—he, a mechanic and she, a homemaker raising two children. At some point they pulled up stakes and moved to New Mexico where they became owners of the Frontier Museum just west of Cuervo.

This was the 1950s when cowboy movies and radio programs were all the rage. Roy Rogers and Dale Evans, Gene Autry, Tom Mix, and the Lone Ranger sparked the imagination of countless children. The Wilsons wisely decided to capitalize on this craze with a Wild West theme consisting of a Wild West Trading Post, the Frontier Museum, a Gay '90s Bar, a cafe, and a service station.

Children, of course, wanted to dress up like their cowboy heroes. To satisfy those fantasies, the Trading Post stocked cowboy hats, Hopalong Cassidy chaps, cap guns and holsters, Western shirts, and best of all—Acme boots. The Museum, on the other hand, was packed with real and fake frontier items, plus ten horse-drawn wagons hitched out front.

Under the guidance of Hondo Marchand, an exact replica of a Concord Stagecoach was built in Albuquerque. This became a featured attraction at the Trading Post. In his youth Hondo had traveled with Will Rogers and his Wild West show learning some of Rogers's trick roping stunts. Hondo drove the stagecoach around the grounds giving rides to weary travelers and cranky kids tired of hours in the back seat of a car with no air conditioning. In 1959, however, Hondo took the stagecoach and left for Indiana where he started giving rides and performing roping tricks in a supermarket parking lot.

One year after Hondo's departure, the Wilsons retired and put the place up for sale. Unfortunately there were no buyers and the buildings were boarded up for years. When Lucy passed away in 1977, all of the contents of the Museum went up for sale. An orthodontist from Southern California bought everything—including the horse-drawn wagons. It took ten trailers to haul all the paraphernalia back to Santa Clarita where many of the items wound up decorating his dental offices.

Sometime after William passed away in 1986, the abandoned buildings burned down. The Frontier Museum had a short life but it was a great stop for Route 66 travelers—especially the kids.

While on a tour of the nearby Bell Ranch several years ago, I met a local rancher who told me that the Gay '90s Bar was a "rip-roaring place" at one time. He didn't mention if he had frequented the establishment.

Santa Rosa
Exits 277, 275, 273 off I-40

"City of Natural Lakes" — in the Desert?

Santa Rosa is "The City of Natural Lakes"— in a desert! These lakes, an oasis for this region, have attracted humans over the centuries. First came Native American bands, then tribes, then the Spanish followed by US settlers.

In 1540 Coronado's expedition, searching for the fabled Seven Cities of Gold, forded the Pecos River—the future site of Santa Rosa—on their return to Mexico empty handed.

In the early 1800s, after the US Army subdued the Native Kiowans, Kiowa Apache, and Comanches, settlers were able to stake out land for farming and ranching in the surrounding area. It wasn't until 1865 that a settlement was established—a Spanish rancho called *Agua Negra Chiquita* (Little Black Water).

By 1868 the community had a post office, and in 1890 was officially named Santa Rosa by Don Celso Baca, the town founder. To honor his mother Rosa, he built a chapel in 1879 naming it Santa Rosa de Lima. The ruins of the chapel and his home across the street can be seen on South Third Street. The cornerstone was laid for a new St. Rose of Lima Catholic Church on the corner of South Third and Lake Drive in 1907. The Church is still in use today.

One of Santa Rosa's claims to fame is the "Blue Hole." Sink holes have formed the lakes in this area, with the Blue Hole being unusual because of its 81-foot depth and its 62 degree crystal clear water. If New Mexicans want to become certified for scuba diving, this is where they train and take their final test.

Santa Rosa has connections with American literary arts, too. Acclaimed author Rudolfo Anaya of the Southwest classic *Bless Me Ultima*, spent his early childhood here and is honored with a park in his name. When the classic movie, *The Grapes of Wrath,* was being filmed in 1940, the bridge in town was used for the train scene.

In 1957 the Sahara Restaurant and Lounge was purchased by Leo and Violet McCowan who had lived in Saudi Arabia for awhile. They served food and libations for twenty years. After the building was boarded up for some time, the neon sign was removed in 2019 and now resides in Albuquerque for restoration. Once repaired, it will glow again in the Glorieta Station Museum—soon to open in downtown Albuquerque.

When travel on Route 66 was at its peak, Santa Rosa featured sixty gas stations, twenty motels, and fifteen restaurants. Today Santa Rosa continues to coax travelers off I-40 with plenty of places to eat, gas up, spend the night, and visit historic sites along its stretch of the Mother Road.

The Route 66 Auto Museum on the old Route is a must-see for aficionados. Along with hundreds of Route 66 souvenirs to peruse, you can pay $5 to see the vintage car showroom, featuring more than thirty restored, mint condition vehicles. Owner Bozo Cordova completes the restorations in his shop across the street while his wife Anna manages the Museum.

And for fun, stop by Joseph's Bar and Grill, stick your face in the *Sproftacchel* by the front door, and get a picture of yourself riding a red convertible down America's Main Street.

St. Rose of Lima Catholic Church on the corner of South Third and Lake Drive, built in 1907.

Part II
Narratives

Route 66 Pre-1937: "The Santa Fe Loop"

From Santa Rosa to Los Ranchos de Albuquerque

Dilia
San Jose
Santa Fe
Santo Domingo
Algodones
Bernalillo

Dilia

Exit 256 from I-40, North on US-84

First Stop on the Santa Fe Loop

Nineteen miles west of Santa Rosa along Interstate 40, one can turn north onto US Highway 84 to travel the original Route 66 heading to Santa Fe. This portion of Route 66 is known as the Santa Fe Loop.

The first community one encounters on the Loop is Dilia. For almost thirty years, attempts to settle the Dilia area were thwarted by constant Apache and Comanche raids. By 1850 settlers had abandoned the area entirely. However, after the Mexican-American War treaty in 1848, Texas, New Mexico, and Arizona became territories of the United States. This allowed the United States Army to step in and provide protection for settlers and the establishment of safe settlements. Dilia was one of them.

In 1911 a post office opened in Dilia putting the community officially on the map. The post office remained open until 1968 when it was moved to nearby La Loma.

When Route 66 was opened for traffic in 1926, the road was described as rough gravel, sandy, and full of stones. It passed through Dilia and headed north to Santa Fe before turning south to Albuquerque.

There are no services in Dilia now. On the corner of US-84 and NM-119 you'll find a deteriorating liquor store set back from the road and surrounded by weeds. If you follow NM-119 one block west, you'll come to the Sacred Heart Church, also known as the *Sagrado Corazon Iglesia,* built in 1900. It is still active, well kept, and a great photo op.

San Jose

Exit 319 off I-25 to Frontage Road 2116
Right on Buffalo Lane (B41D)

Pecos River Crossing

San Jose's roots extend back to 1794 when the Spanish military and a colony of *Genizaros* from Santa Fe camped along the Pecos River. *Genizaros* were captured Native Americans who had been sold as slaves to the Spanish and converted to Catholicism. As a result, when freed, their former tribes rejected them. Rather than allow them to remain in Santa Fe, the governor moved the *Genizaros* to the east of the city where he hoped they would act as a buffer from raiding Comanches and Apaches arriving from the eastern plains.

The official town of San Jose was founded along the west bank of the Pecos River in 1803 when 47 people—two were women—were given parcels of land by the Spanish government. When the Santa Fe Trail opened in 1821, travelers and caravans full of trade goods crossed the river at San Jose. Five years later, permission was given by the Bishop of Durango to build a church on the town's plaza.

Twenty years after that, during the Mexican-American War (1846–1848), United States Army General Stephen Kearney marched through San Jose, declaring this area part of America. On the heels of the American acquisition of this formerly Spanish-Mexican territory, stagecoach service arrived from Independence, Missouri, by way of the Santa Fe Trail. This was followed by mail service, and finally, in 1858, a post office. That same year, train tracks were laid to the north bypassing San Jose. As so frequently happened, the community declined from lack of commerce.

San Jose was revived in 1926 with the construction of Route 66. Cars now traveled through town, crossing the river on a steel truss bridge. As fate would have it, Route 66 was rerouted in 1937, bypassing San Jose and the entire northern Santa Fe Loop. The community languished again, the road became overgrown, and the bridge fell into disuse. Although it still stands today with its weathered wooden planks, it's a bridge to nowhere.

As of 2010, the population of San Jose was 137. The church still anchors the center of town, with a small post office nearby. No other services are available.

In 1910 the Daughters of the American Revolution installed several stone markers in New Mexico commemorating the Santa Fe Trail. This one is located in San Jose, just west of the bridge that crosses the Pecos River.

Santa Fe

Exit 282B off I-25, North on St. Francis Drive

The City Different: A Historical Landmark

The history of La Fonda Hotel **is** the history of Santa Fe.

The La Fonda Hotel in Santa Fe is an old—but refurbished—grand lady. Over 400 years ago the Spanish built the first inn on this corner of the Plaza in 1607. *La Fonda* means "The Inn" and as people kept referring to it as "the Inn," the name La Fonda stuck.

The first overland party of Americans to reach Santa Fe was led by Captain William Becknell. Departing Independence, Missouri, in 1821, his mission was to establish a trade route connecting Missouri to Santa Fe that became known as the Santa Fe Trail. When the party arrived in Santa Fe, they enjoyed a restful stay at La Fonda.

As time went on, La Fonda became the inn of choice for gold miners, trappers, businessmen, and politicians alike. When Route 66 reached Santa Fe it followed the Old Santa Fe Trail to the San Miguel Mission, crossed the Santa Fe River, passed the Loretto Chapel and the front door of La Fonda Hotel, before heading south on Water Street. The hotel burned down in 1920 and was rebuilt in 1922 in the Spanish Pueblo Style.

In 1925 the Atchison, Topeka and Santa Fe Railroad bought the hotel and promptly leased its operation to Fred Harvey. The chain of Harvey Houses across the Southwest was famous for its food and lodging as well as the Harvey Girls who served the customers. Architect Mary Coulter redesigned the interiors of La Fonda adding Spanish and Mexican tile, stained glass, tin chandeliers, and carved ceiling *vigas*.

Fred Harvey operated La Fonda until 1968 when a local group purchased the hotel and continues to manage it today. The traditional interior is dramatic with high-end shops and galleries lining the hallways. Centrally located off the lobby, skylights brighten *La Plazuela*, an elegant, indoor dining patio. The ambiance is relaxed and the food is excellent. Reservations are a good idea.

Hand painted glass panes of the doors and windows enclose the charming La Plazuela dining area at La Fonda.

Elegant shops located within La Fonda display distinctive Southwestern items.

174

Santa Fe

Exit 282B off I-25 to St. Francis Drive, Left on Cerrillos Road

Route 66 Vintage Motels

During the heyday of the Santa Fe Loop, people traveled to Santa Fe and south to Albuquerque. Travelers and sightseers arrived in the city, famed for its culture and the romance of the West.

For some, Santa Fe was a destination. For others, it was a gateway to the art and literary scene at Taos—the world of Mabel Dodge Lujan, D. H. Lawrence, and Georgia O'Keeffe. The need for more lodging in Santa Fe became apparent. (Even my parents rendezvoused in Santa Fe—my dad on a motor trip and my mother by train from San Francisco. She wrote in her diary that while they were in Taos, they stayed at a motel for $1.25 a night. When I did the math, I discovered they must have been unmarried at the time.)

Along Route 66 in Santa Fe (Cerrillos Road) are several surviving lodging places. El Rey Court opened in 1936 with twelve guest rooms. When the Santa Fe Cut-Off to Albuquerque was paved in 1937, travelers going through New Mexico bypassed Santa Fe. However, the El Rey Court survived the declining traffic as Santa Fe continued to grow as a tourist attraction. By 1973, thirty-eight rooms had been added to accommodate the interest in Santa Fe's art galleries, Southwest archaeology, numerous world-class museums, and frequent special events like Indian Market.

Today the El Rey has eighty-six guest rooms. Featuring original art, Navajo rugs, antiques, and Western-styled furniture, each room is uniquely different. Even the grounds, with its charming walkways and gardens, large shade trees, and swimming pool, continue to shelter guests from the bustle of Cerrillos Road.

In 2016 Jeff Burns and Matt Comfort purchased the El Rey. Jay and Allison Carroll, as managing co-partners, continue to redesign the grounds and rooms. They've added a lounge where locals frequent this historic establishment for cocktails, enjoying the warmth of a large fireplace in winter and refreshing breezes on the lawn during the summer months.

King's Rest Court and the Cottonwood Court Motel are also vintage Route 66 places to stay along Cerrillos Road. Survivors of good times and bad, these lodgings have been updated and modernized for today's travelers and Mother Road enthusiasts.

Santo Domingo Trading Post

Exit 259 off I-25
Turn right onto 22. Follow the signs.

"Where Real Indians Trade"

In 1881, midway between Santa Fe and Albuquerque, a trading post was built in the former town of Domingo. It supplied groceries, clothing, and farm supplies to the locals, Pueblo residents, and ranchers in the area. The Seligman family acquired the property in 1922, converted the original building to a warehouse and constructed a new two-story adobe trading post in the Mission Revival style.

When Route 66 came along, the road ran between the trading post and the Santa Fe Railroad tracks, a great location for business. The brightly painted signs on the buildings declaring the trading post as "The Most Interesting Spot in the Old West…Where Real Indians Trade" attracted tourists seeking Native American jewelry, pottery, and Southwestern curios.

However, when the Route 66 Santa Fe Loop was bypassed at the end of 1926, travelers sped directly from

Santa Rosa to Albuquerque on the new Santa Fe Cut-Off. Tourist trade dwindled at the Santo Domingo Trading Post and other places enroute to Albuquerque.

In 1946 Fred Thompson took over the business and operated it until his passing in 1995 when it was closed. He catered mostly to the Pueblo tribe and other local residents, providing groceries, mercantile provisions, and gasoline. The trading post's national claim to fame occurred when it was featured in a 1943 *Life Magazine* article and again in 1962 when visited by presidential candidate on the stump—John F. Kennedy.

In 1998 this 127 year old, former commercial trading post was added to the National Register of Historic Places. Sadly, in 2001, the buildings caught fire and were mostly destroyed. Only the facades were spared. Fortunately the National Park Service and its Route 66 Corridor Preservation Program provided a million dollar grant to rebuild the trading post. Santo Domingo artist Ricardo Cate restored the artwork on the facade. The trading post is now operated by the Kewa Pueblo, selling fine arts, crafts, and jewelry created by Native American artisans of New Mexico.

To get there by car, take the Santo Domingo exit 259 off I-25 and follow the signs. Or take the train: The trading post is across the street from the Kewa Rail Runner Station.

Algodones
Exit 248 off I-25

Stone's Buffalo Trading Post, aka Rosa's Cantina

Mention Rosa's Cantina and folks only seem to recall the murder of a young woman committed there in 1975. However, if asked about the history of Stone's Buffalo Trading Post, they provide only a blank stare.

In 1946 John Stone was named as the owner of this store in an advertisement for Indian jewelry, rugs, and crafts sold at his establishment. The store may have carried some supplies for the local residents and customers from the nearby pueblo. The curio shop was an eye-catcher, with colorful paintings on the exterior walls and an *horno,* fake Indian pottery, and carved wooden Kachinas set outside on the premises.

The next account I found was in 1972 when robbers broke into the shop, beating John to the floor, holding a gun to his wife's head, and running off with hundreds of dollars worth of silver and turquoise jewelry.

When Rosa's Cantina opened up in an adjacent building, it quickly became a hot spot. University of New Mexico students, bikers, and partiers alike congregated on weekends for a rollicking time of drinking and dancing, all to the tune of local bands. A friend of mine remembers having a wild time there one Saturday evening— right after her divorce was final.

With the discovery of the missing girl's body thrown in the irrigation ditch behind the cantina, the Buffalo Trading Post was put up for sale. By 1976 the atmosphere and the clientele changed for the better. It became a stop for tourists looking for locally made silver jewelry, woven rugs, and pottery. The business eventually closed and the location was just another place by the side of the road.

In June of 2022 I drove by this place and could hardly believe my eyes. The grounds were cleared of brush, and the cluster of

One of the original paintings on Stone's Buffalo Trading Post exterior walls, still visible today.

buildings were painted bright white with handsome natural wood trim on the doors and windows. The rug paintings on the back building are now beautifully restored to their original colorful designs.

I was astonished and thrilled, since often I return to sites where the original murals on buildings are fading, the roofs are caving in, and the walls are crumbling. Coming across this site, I felt hopeful for the renewed interest in preserving historical Route 66 places such as this.

Bernalillo
Exit 240 off I-25

Silva's Saloon—A Family History

The Silva family has been a part of Bernalillo since 1905 when a Syrian trader by the name of Ferris Shaheen settled here. He opened a general store and saloon and married Dolores Gallegos from nearby Algodones. Sometime during those early years he changed his name to Silva (the Shaheen name didn't fit into his adopted community). He died in 1928. Four years later his oldest son George was murdered at the age of twenty-two. Many felt it was a hate crime, and the ballad "El Corrido de George Silva – a Bernalillo Tragedy" resulted.

A younger son, James Silva, and his wife Ella continued the family tradition of trading with Native American artists, opening a store next to the saloon in 1933. They traded with some of the great Indian artists of the century including Cochiti Storyteller clay artist Helen Cordero, sculptor and painter Allan Houser, and Navajo painter and printmaker Harrison Begay.

By 1970 James and Ella had purchased the entire complex which included the saloon, a theater, a trading post, drugstore, auto parts store, and gas station. The complex has seen many incarnations including The Range Cafe, which has enhanced the historic building's place as a local landmark and popular restaurant. The couple raised six children including Rose, who continues to operate Rose's Pottery House next to the Range Cafe. The space formerly used as a theater now serves as a kind of museum and tribute to the Silva family. If you ask nicely, you may be able to see it.

Another son, Felix Silva Sr., a moonshiner and bootlegger during Prohibition, opened Silva's Saloon in Bernalillo in 1933, one day after prohibition ended. Even then, this enterprise may not have been a completely legitimate one. There were rumors of Sunday liquor sales, alcohol sold to Native Americans (both illegal at the time), and illicit card games going on. Felix Sr. worked the bar every day, and his son Felix Jr. eventually began working at the saloon when old enough to serve customers.

The tales and memories are endless. That Felix Sr. kept nine guns around the bar for protection is true. However, the only known altercation involved a fellow being bopped on the head with a pipe. The blood specks on the ceiling can still be seen. That a CIA agent used the old pay telephone to call headquarters is also true. Despite these stories, the father-son business had little tolerance for bad manners at their establishment and enforced their set of proprietary rules.

The saloon is still a regular stop for locals while its history attracts many visitors as well. The walls of the bar are decorated with odd mementos, old license plates, layered newspaper clippings yellowed with age, and fading pictures of events and patrons. Above the wall of available liquid refreshments is a row of old, unopened bottles that have been around since the 1930s. Each was dipped in wax a long time ago to preserve its contents.

Motorcycle groups enjoy reserved parking out front of Silva's. To outsiders, all the bikes lined up in front of the saloon might scare them off from entering this local watering hole. However, the Silva code of conduct keeps it a friendly stop for all who enter. If you're lucky, maybe you'll stop by when it's Cowboy Poetry Night.

In 1995 Felix Jr. discovered his father passed away in the bar. Nowadays Denise Silva, a retired public school teacher, tends bar at the saloon, cares for her father Felix Jr., and runs a tight ship at Silva's Saloon, continuing the family tradition.

Essay by Joan Fenicle

Part III
Narratives

Route 66 Post-1937: "The Santa Fe Cut-Off"

Clines Corners Rest Stop
The Longhorn Ranch
The Hitching Post
Moriarty
Midway Trading Post
Edgewood
Albuquerque

Clines Corners Rest Stop

Exit 218 off I-40

Moving with the Road

Roy Cline was an expert mover. In 1926 he moved his family of six daughters and one son from Arkansas to New Mexico. They first settled near Moriarty where he tried his hand at farming. When that effort failed, he tried the hotel business in town. That, too, fared no better. He then moved a few miles south to Lucy, New Mexico, where he opened a hamburger joint and service station. That location wasn't ideal. So he moved the buildings north to the Route 66 dirt road at the junction of Highway 6 and Highway 2.

In 1937 Route 66 was realigned and now his business was south of this major highway. Once again he literally picked up buildings and all, resettling them at its present location near I-40. He soon opened a gas station and cafe and the place became known as Clines Corners.

Business was slow at first. To save a penny, Cline kept the lights off until he saw a car approaching. The lights glowed for as long as the travelers were in the shop. Then he'd switch them off as the customers drove away. He charged ten cents for a gallon of gas. For a gallon of water, he charged $1.00, because water had to be hauled by truck from Estancia Valley forty miles away.

In 1939 Cline sold his business to S. Lynn "Smitty" Smith who invested time and money upgrading the establishment. Over the years the business changed hands several times. Once again, Roy Cline moved on, starting several ventures in Arizona and New Mexico.

If you stop at the present-day Clines Corners, you can fill up with gas and food and use the clean restrooms. You'll find 3,000 square feet crammed with every Southwestern souvenir imaginable. Over one million people stop here every year and many walk out clutching a couple of curios and a New Mexico T-shirt.

The Longhorn Ranch

Exit 203 off I-40

Where the West Once Lived

Located east of Moriarty, The Longhorn Ranch went from boom to bust in thirty-seven years.

In the late 1930s, William "Bill" Ehret, a former policeman from Endicott, New York, became a New Mexico State Police officer assigned to Lincoln County. His beat covered 5,000 square miles south of Moriarty. Patrolling such a vast territory meant little time for home and family.

By 1937 the Santa Fe Cut-Off running straight west from Santa Rosa to Albuquerque was improved. During Ehret's long days covering this rural area, he noticed many more people using this east-west roadway. He also noticed that there were long stretches with few opportunities to purchase food and gas along the route. Ehret made a career change.

He bought land seven miles east of Moriarty, settled his family there, and immediately built a ten-stool cafe and curio shop. His business opened in 1940 and rode the wave of the Cowboy Culture craze popularized first in cinema and then on television. He christened his enterprise The Longhorn Ranch.

As post-World War II travel increased, the ranch expanded to include stagecoach rides, a Western museum, Indian dances, a saloon, an eighteen room hotel, a garage, and a longhorn cow named "Babe." Billed as "Where the Spirit of the Old West Still Lives," the ranch became a popular stop. In fact, it ended up looking like a film set for Western movies.

In 1955 Ehret sold The Longhorn Ranch and moved on. The new owners ran the business until 1977 when I-40 bypassed the ranch.

Like so many Western ghost towns, Babe's home today is a pile of rubble with a bent sign creaking and swaying in the afternoon winds.

(The source for much of this information comes from "Story of the Longhorn Ranch on New Mexico Route 66" posted on MrZip66.com.)

The Hitching Post
Exit 196 off I-40
East on Abrahames Road, just past Perimeter Rd

Snakes and Souvenirs

John Claar, an Ohio native with past careers in speed boat racing and working the carnival circuit, headed West in 1947. With his brother-in-law Jack Gibson, he landed in Milagro, New Mexico, where the Guiles family ran a successful gas station along Route 66. To increase business, the Guiles had gathered local wild animals, caged them, and called it a zoo. However, the favorite attraction was the snake pit. Tourists literally lined up for a chance to watch real live rattlesnakes.

Noticing the expanding tourist trade, John and Jack set up their own gig of carnival games across the road from the Guiles family business. John quickly put his barker skills to profitable use. His flair for showmanship and snake-oil charm easily encouraged visitors to part with their money.

As traffic increased, John Claar decided to cash in on the vacation boom. He bought a souvenir shop and gas station near Moriarty in 1950 and promptly named it The Hitching Post.

Next he added a zoo. Recalling the real money-maker, he built a snake pit and filled it full of diamondback rattlers. Signs dubbed it "The Den of Death." Tourists were encouraged to throw money into the pit and make a wish that would surely—with a wink—come true. John's son Don remembers that every spring he would scrape out the coins. After washing and rolling them, he and his sister counted hundreds of dollars collected in a season.

John also sold lots of Southwestern souvenirs, claiming they were made by American Indians. Meanwhile, his kids were in a back room, scraping off "Made in Japan" labels from the latest shipment.

The Hitching Post thrived until John had a stroke. His wife passed away, and the business was leased to a family friend. After I-40 was completed and traffic redirected, The Hitching Post closed for good in 1967. It is still owned by the Claar family.

The original SNAKE PIT still stands, sturdy as ever. One is compelled to take a peek, cautiously, to see if there's a rattlesnake slithering around inside beneath the metal grating.

Hand painted Southwestern vignettes can still be seen on the exterior walls of the Hitching Post

Moriarty

Exits 197, 196, 194 off I-40

Home of the "Pinto Bean Fiesta"

Rheumatism, aggravated by bitter Iowa winters, drove Michael Moriarty from his farm in 1887. With his wife and three kids, he began homesteading an isolated section of New Mexico east of the Sandia Mountains. Since there was no post office, mail was delivered by horseback from Chilili, approximately ten miles away.

Isolation ended, however, when the railroad arrived in 1903. A post office was established, and Michael Moriarty became the first postmaster. The settlement was named after him and blossomed as the train brought homesteaders from the Midwest to ranch and dry farm the fertile soil.

The town grew until the early 1930s when the Great Depression hit. Along with drought and storms spewing grit from the Dust Bowl, the once excellent farm land was ruined. Without rain, crops withered. Farmers were forced to abandon the area seeking jobs elsewhere. Moriarty's population and businesses spiraled downward.

However, in 1937 things began looking up. The new Route 66 alignment, running straight from Santa Rosa to Albuquerque, cruised down Moriarty's Main Street. This invigorated the town as tourists motoring east and west needed gas and accommodations. By 1950 Moriarty had thriving motels, cafes, bars, repair shops, and eleven gas stations. It even held dances every Saturday night. This boom lasted until the 1970s, when I-40 was built and bypassed Moriarty. As a result, Moriarty lost much of its tourist trade.

What has endured is a vibrant ranching community sponsoring its Pinto Bean Fiesta, Fourth of July celebrations, and a busy community center.

As for Route 66 attractions, Moriarty is home to a preserved Whiting Brothers Gas Station. For car lovers, the Lewis Auto and Toy Museum houses beautifully restored automobiles in a large building. You can also wander among acres of vintage vehicles and rusting parts lodged among the weeds in the back. (Watch out for snakes!) Lewis will never be bored, having several lifetimes of restoration ahead of him.

Then there's the local RETRO 66 group, actively preserving Route 66—its buildings and history—and promoting its lore to America and the world.

A Route 66 sculpture made of car parts. 2022

Midway Trading Post

I-40 Exit 187 to Route 66, east of Edgewood

A Restored Photo Op

Located about 171 miles into New Mexico—halfway between Texas and Arizona—the Midway Trading Post was built in 1945. Sporting the usual gas station, cafe, and curio shop, its unique feature was an *horno*, the Spanish word for an outdoor adobe oven. It was built to show tourists how Pueblo women baked bread.

The trading post soon became a community center, a post office, and a municipal court which served the surrounding residents. Like many other stops and shops along Route 66, it closed in 1972, another casualty of the new I-40 highway. Standing abandoned for years, the building became a target for graffiti artists and spray paint purchasers.

In 2013 the RETRO 66 Relive the Route Committee located in Edgewood, New Mexico, decided to reclaim the building and convert it into a tourist attraction and photo op for Route 66 aficionados. High school students from Moriarty and Edgewood and other volunteers—sixty in all— showed up during June 2013 to clean up the premises. They ripped down the fence, cleared the encroaching weeds and brush, and painted over the heavily graffitied walls. The boxcar got a fresh paint job, as well. Local artist Willy Fisher painted all the signage.

The *horno* is still there, although no longer baking bread, restored for more snapshot opportunities.

The outdoor adobe *horno* provides a great photo op.

Edgewood

Exit 187 off I-40

West on North Frontage Road to Wildlife West Nature Park

Finding the Red Top Diner

While cruising a section of Route 66 just east of Edgewood, I spotted a Red Top Diner parked alongside the road. I immediately stopped, reached for my camera, and took its photo against a cloudless sky.

Ten days later when the sky was filled with billowing clouds, I drove back to take a few more shots. Gone. Nothing there. Only the pad it had been resting on remained.

For several years I scanned the internet, hoping to discover what had happened to that Red Top Diner. Serendipitously, while enjoying a hamburger at the Route 66 Diner on Central Avenue in Albuquerque, I started a conversation with a Mother Road enthusiast. I mentioned my search for the mysterious disappearance of the Red Top Diner.

A vintage advertising door handle.

He chuckled and explained, "Oh, that. It's on display at the Wildlife West Nature Park near Edgewood." Mystery solved.

About the Valentine Diners

As the Great Depression deepened, Valentine diners were the brainchild of Arthur Valentine. Prefabricated in Wichita, Kansas, they could be ordered through a catalogue.

The first one was built around 1932. Arthur wanted them to be affordable ($5,000) and transportable. They were rectangular in design, the size of a box car, and could be loaded onto a train or trailer to be shipped anywhere in the United States. The diner came fully equipped with a grill, counter top, stools, shelves, etc. In a couple of hours a new food outlet could be set up and ready to serve customers. In fact, only one or two persons were needed to run these diners. They were the forerunner of today's fast-food restaurants.

After 1970, however, the demand for a quick, inexpensive meal shifted away from such diners in favor of drive-through food businesses. As McDonald's and other fast-food franchises rose in popularity and cornered the market, the need for Valentine Diners declined until they were no longer being built.

A few remnants of these diners, however, still exist around New Mexico. Interestingly, the Little House Diner was moved to Girard and Central in 1997 and converted into a police substation next to the University of New Mexico—a Valentine Diner in disguise—right in downtown Albuquerque.

Albuquerque

Cruise the entire length of Route 66 through Albuquerque along Central Avenue, between exits 167 and 149 off of I-40.

The KiMo: An Iconic Theater

If the glowing red-eyed buffalo skulls lining the proscenium don't spook you a little, then the repeated swastika motif will certainly get your attention. But, relax. They are just a small part of the extravagant Pueblo Deco style of the KiMo Theatre on Central Avenue—*aka* Route 66—in downtown Albuquerque.

The KiMo Theatre was the vision of Oreste Bachechi, a newcomer to the Southwest, who arrived in the United States in 1885. He established a business housed in a tent near the train tracks in Albuquerque. As the city grew, so did his entrepreneurship, with the operation of various stores and a theater.

Thinking that Albuquerque needed an entertainment palace, Bachechi dreamt of an iconic theater and spent $150,000 to construct one designed by Carl Boller of Boller Brothers who specialized in theater architecture. Boller studied Pueblo designs for months, visiting nearby pueblos, before submitting a watercolor rendition of his vision—a melding of the then popular Art Deco style geometrics with motifs from local Native American cultures.

As such, there are plaster ceiling beams painted to look like logs (*vigas*) decorated with dance and hunting scenes. Air vents were disguised as Navajo rugs, and wrought iron long-necked birds served as door handles. Those backwards swastikas are also Native American symbols for life, freedom, and happiness. To complete the interior, nine large wall murals were painted by artist Carl Von Hassler. Like Michelangelo before him, Von Hassler spent months on twenty-foot-high scaffolds to complete the scenes. Lastly, an $18,000 pipe organ was installed to

Pueblo Deco details of the KiMo Theatre.

accompany the silent movies when the doors opened for business in 1927. Bachechi died one year later.

After a contest, the winning name, KiMo, was submitted by Governor Pablo Abeita of Isleta Pueblo who collected the $50 prize money. *KiMo*, a Tiwa word, means mountain lion. Over the years, the theater changed hands many times. The buffalo skulls may have blushed a bit when the theater briefly became a venue for adult films. Then, in 1963 when a fire severely damaged much of the stage, the theater was scheduled for demolition.

The citizens of Albuquerque, however, rallied and urged the city to purchase the building and return the theater to its glory days. The renovated theater, added to the National Register of Historic Places in 1977, now has seating for 660 and is in continuous use for movies and live performances.

Then there's the presence of two ghosts. One is a six-year-old lad, Bobby Darnell, who was killed in 1951 when the theater boiler exploded. He is known for playing pranks on the likes of Vivian Vance of *I Love Lucy* television fame, feather fan dancer Sally Rand, and movie stars Gloria Swanson, Tom Mix, and Ginger Rogers. The other ghost is a mysterious, unknown woman who benignly strolls the hallways. They're just another facet of the KiMo's long history.

The KiMo Theatre, located at 423 Central Avenue NW, remains the City of Albuquerque's iconic arts and culture venue, with an emphasis on art, film, and theater performances. Nestled in the heart of Albuquerque, the KiMo Theatre is a time capsule of Route 66—then and now.

Essay contributed by Dorothy E. Noe

Maisel's Historic Indian Trading Post

When Route 66 was rerouted bypassing the Santa Fe Loop, the Mother Road became Central Avenue traveling right through downtown Albuquerque.

Maurice Maisel, an astute businessman, noticed more tourists were now in the Duke City and seemed fascinated by Indian Country and Indian-made merchandise. Sensing an opportunity, he decided to capitalize on this interest with a storefront at 510 Central Avenue.

Maisel had two criteria for the look of his new storefront: a modern appearance employing elements of the then popular Art Deco style to attract travelers, and a showcase for the Indian wares that were on the shelves.

To create this combination, he employed John Gaw Meem, the famous Santa Fe architect credited with the revival of Pueblo style buildings. Meem, in turn, sought out Olive Rush, an art teacher at the Santa Fe Indian School, to decorate the façade of his structure. Rush hired her best students, paying them $5 a day, to create seventeen murals. Many of these painters—Pablita Verlarde, Pop Chalee, Popovi Da—went on to become recognized artists in their own right.

By the 1940s and through the 1950s Maisel's store employed over 300 Navajo and Pueblo artists and craftsmen, becoming the largest operation of its kind. In 1960, however, Maurice died and the store was closed until the 1980s, when his grandson reopened the business under the banner "Skip Maisel's Indian Jewelry & Crafts."

Skip made some renovations to the building and above the front door installed a glowing neon sign of a feathered Indian head. He spent his tenure at the store traveling to various Indian reservations to purchase handmade jewelry, pottery, rugs, and other fine crafts to stock his business.

In 1993 Maisel's Indian Trading Post was added to the National Register of Historic Places. Skip operated Maisel's until early 2019 when he retired to relax and care for his horses.

After months of storewide sales that emptied the shelves, the building was purchased by the Garcia Automotive Group. Carlos Garcia has vowed to preserve its historic character. At this writing, he has not decided what to do with the building but is not in any rush.

The Maisel storefront murals are still visible, attracting fans of John Gaw Meem's architecture and Route 66 enthusiasts alike. Sadly, the distinctive Indian head neon sign over Maisel's has disappeared.

On a personal note: Whenever my parents visited me from California, they made a pilgrimage to Maisel's where my father could always find the perfect anniversary gift for my mother—a concho belt, a squash blossom necklace, or turquoise bracelet—which she immediately and joyfully put on to display.

The "City of Neon" on Route 66

One of the great rewards of moseying through the towns along Route 66 in New Mexico is to experience the outstanding array of vintage neon signs.

Neon signage evolved into an art form after World War II when tourism boomed and travelers hit the road looking for adventure, entertainment, and memory-making moments. Route 66 evolved as the most famous road in America, offering 2,400 miles of sights, scenery, and fun from Chicago to Los Angeles.

With countless tourists on the road, there was money to be made providing travelers with food, gas, and lodging. Added to that were roadside attractions, trading posts, and curio shops. Enterprising business owners realized they needed a hook to entice motorists to actually slow down and pull into their establishments. Neon signs fulfilled that need, and the art of neon took off.

Unlike anywhere else on Route 66, New Mexico's neon enchanted and charmed travelers. Cowboys, bucking broncos, Indians, cactus, and conquistadors outlined in luminous strands of dazzling emerald greens, ruby reds, sapphire blues, and pearly white glowed in the night skies.

Even today neon continues to light up Historic Route 66 in New Mexico. Look for it at the Blue Swallow Motel and the Tepee Curio Shop in Tucumcari; the La Loma and La Mesa motels in Santa Rosa; the Sands Motel and West Theatre in Grants; and in Gallup, the Blue Spruce Lodge and El Rancho Hotel.

The longest run of neon can still be found cruising the sixteen miles of Old Route 66 along Central Avenue that traverses the heart of Albuquerque. Long recognized for its opulent array of neon, Albuquerque was proclaimed on old postcards as the "City of Neon." One such postcard noted, "Albuquerque is reputed to have the most brightly lighted main street in America. This galaxy of neon makes it an easily believable fact."

Cruising along Route 66, New Mexico has it all when it comes to classic neon signage. From weathered and worn relics still standing proudly at their original sites to artfully restored neon and newly inspired retro styled neon—each is a delight to discover.

Essay by Johnnie Meier

To experience New Mexico rock art, visit Petroglyph National Monument located on Albuquerque's westside.

Part IV
Narratives

From Albuquerque to Milan

Suwanee-Correo
Budville
Villa de Cubero Trading Post
San Fidel
Whiting Brothers
Grants
Milan

Suwanee–Correo
Exit 126 off I-40

Wild Times at the Wild Horse Mesa Bar

The community of Suwanee and the Correo Trading Post are separated by the railroad tracks. In Spanish *correo* means "mail" and the local post office was housed in the trading post. Needless to say, the residents of Suwanee had to cross the overpass to retrieve their mail. While there, they could also pick up groceries and observe the occasional tourist surveying the collection of Navajo rugs and turquoise jewelry on display for sale.

Today just a few crumbling walls and foundations remain of the trading post located west of the tracks near NM-6 and I-40. On the east side of the tracks is the small settlement, now referred to as Suwanee. Back in the 1950s the names were interchangeable.

Henry Andrews Jr. ran the trading post and curio shop. By the mid 1940s he had added a small cafe and a few cabins for rent out back. In front were gas pumps that served Route 66 travelers and the residents from the surrounding area. You can still see the cement island where the pumps once stood.

Jake Atkinson, who ran the Rattle Snake Trading Post near Bluewater and various tourist businesses around the State, came to town in the late 1950s. He opened a bar/restaurant across the tracks from the trading post that attracted serious drinkers from the local area. Unfortunately, there was bad blood between these drinkers that resulted in extremely brutal fights.

The now defunct Wild Horse Mesa Bar may, in fact, be this very same "bucket-o-blood" bar. A reference to Correo can be found in Thomas Repp's book, *Route 66, The Romance of the West* (page 28).

Budville
Exit 104 off I-40

Murder and Mayhem on Route 66

Budville, New Mexico, owes its existence to U. S. Route 66. In 1936 Howard Neil "Bud" Rice opened a general store, gas station, and towing service about fifty-five miles west of Albuquerque along that famous road.

At various times Rice served as Justice of the Peace and Valencia County deputy sheriff while also operating an Indian pawn business and an automobile salvage yard. As justice of the peace, he assessed fines so excessive—on out-of-state speeders especially—that Budville was placed on the American Automobile Association (AAA) national speed-trap list in the 1960s.

Rice was well known for his long-standing opposition to the construction of Interstate 40. He managed to keep it from opening for several years until it finally bypassed his town in early 1968.

The village, at most, along with Rice's trading post, amounted to two bars, two churches, and one restaurant. There were no houses in Budville. The dozen or so residents lived on the premises of businesses they operated. One mobile home arrived in the 1970s.

Rice and an elderly employee were shot to death in the Budville trading post on November 18, 1967, during a robbery attempt. While a couple of arrests were made in the case and one man was tried, no one was ever convicted of the crime.

After Bud Rice was killed, his wife Flossie married Max Atkinson. On August 3, 1971, Atkinson's brother

Phil was shot and killed in a gunfight with unknown assailants in front of the Budville trading post. No one was ever arrested for that crime. Max himself was shot and killed by a local rancher on June 7, 1973, in a dispute over the branding of a steer.

As a result of the murders, Budville bar owner Joe Garcia Jr. began calling the town "Bloodville."

Essay by Don Bullis, Author of Bloodville.

Villa de Cubero Trading Post

Exit 104 off I-40

Fame, Fortune, and Pickles

What do novelist Ernest Hemingway, Vivian Vance of television fame, Route 66, and the Villa de Cubero Trading Post have in common? It's quite a tale.

In 1936, when the two-lane Route 66 was the main street running though the Village of Cubero, Sidney Gottlieb owned the large and prosperous Cubero Trading Company where horse and wagons were hitched next to parked cars. Here he traded goods with the local residents for cattle, sheep, and wool, as well as pottery made by artists from Laguna and Acoma Pueblos.

When parts of Route 66 were about to be straightened out in 1937, Sidney Gottlieb anticipated the Village of Cubero would be cut off the beaten path. Being a smart businessman, the former pickle salesman plunked down $88,000 to build a second store with gas pumps along the new section of Route 66, ready to cater to the ever-increasing tourist trade.

Behind the Trading Post he added a motor court where each room had its own garage. A particular room was pointed out to me where Ernest Hemingway supposedly stayed in 1951 while writing his Pulitzer Prize winning novel *The Old Man and the Sea*. Mary, a Gottlieb relative who cleaned his room, considered him a slob for tossing wine bottles from the window and called him *El Diablo* (The Devil).

In all likelihood, if Hemingway really stayed there, he took his meals across the street at the Villa de Cubero Café run by Mary Gunn, another Gottlieb relative. The menu offered eggs and bacon, enchiladas, and a side of refried beans to be washed down with a thick milkshake that was famous for miles around.

On the other hand, Vivian Vance's connection to the Villa is better documented than Hemingway's. Best remembered for her comic role as Ethel Mertz, Lucille Ball's sidekick in the long-running comedy series *I Love Lucy*, Vance was a longtime resident of New Mexico, having moved from Kansas to Albuquerque with her parents in 1928. Fulfilling her childhood dreams of acting, Vance got her start at the KiMo Theatre performing in vaudeville shows. Although rumor has it that she, too, stayed in the Villa's motel, it is more likely she and her husband stayed at a cabin at the Bibo Ranch in nearby Cubero. Although her thoughts were to retire in the country near Cubero, they never did.

Today the Villa de Cubero Trading Post, now owned by Keith Gottlieb, continues to be a hub of activity. Tourists and locals gas up and dash inside for an ice cream or a six pack. It's truly an old fashioned general store, stocking items from wooden kitchen matches, oil lamps, groceries, and horse shoes to clothespins, toothpaste, and Hershey Bars, along with a fine collection of old pottery displayed in the owner's office. Lining the walls are framed photographs by Laguna Pueblo's famous photographer Lee Marmon. They mingle with the mounted heads of hunted animals. And, of course, in honor of Grandfather Sidney, there's a shelf stocked with large jars of pickles.

Essay by Dorothy E. Noe

San Fidel

Exit 100 off I-40

"Welcome to Geezerville"

San Fidel wasn't always called San Fidel. The first settlers to lay claim to this desolate area west of Laguna were the Baltazar Jaramillo family who arrived in 1868. Needless to say, there were no public buildings at that time. Twenty-four years later, the first community structure—a church—was constructed in 1892. As the population of the area was slow to increase, it took another eighteen years until a post office was opened in 1910. The original name for the community was Ballejos but was changed in 1919 to San Fidel.

By 1916 Abdoo Fidel's Lebanese family had moved into the community and opened the first general store. When Route 66 was commissioned, it ran through the center of town, and Abdoo noticed an influx of tourists traveling through. As an enterprising businessman, he added curios to his store. His niche, however, was to offer pottery produced exclusively by the nearby Acoma Pueblo artisans. As business increased, he moved the curio trade from the general store to the building that still exists. He called his shop Acoma Curios. Some of the pottery for sale was made by the famous Acoma artists Lucy Lewis and Mary Z. Chino.

The Acoma Curios building was an adobe structure with a twist: an "out-of-character" false front was added to mimic a Wild West style fasçade. Business prospered until World War II when gasoline was rationed resulting in fewer travelers and a decline in sales. Adjusting to the times, Fidel converted the curio shop back to selling general merchandise, adding gas pumps, a cafe, and a garage.

At some point Fidel quit the business and Standard Oil acquired the building. Since then, it has changed hands several times. In its last incarnation, it was an art gallery that no longer operates. The building was placed on the National Register of Historic Places in 2009.

The side of the Acoma Curio Shop identifies the building.

Whiting Brothers

Exit 96 off I-40

Gas for Less

In the 1970s, the Whiting Brothers Corporation decided to sell its once popular gas station near San Fidel. There were no buyers. Oddly, even as the station gradually crumbled, it still attracted a following but not for filling gas tanks. Today, people from all over the world stop here year round for photo ops.

When the Whiting Brothers' family opened their first general store in St. Johns, Arizona, they noticed that farmers and ranchers needed gasoline for their equipment. They began stocking gas in five gallon tins. The year was 1917 and marked the beginning of what would become the chain of Whiting Brothers gas stations in operation across the Southwest over the next 70 years. By 1925, with more automobiles in use, gasoline was now in steady demand and gas pumps were added to their store.

The following year Route 66 was established bringing even more motorists in need of fuel. The Whiting brothers expanded the gas station business from their base in Arizona to include California, New Mexico, and Texas, concentrating their stations along the popular Route 66. At the high point of their business expansion, there were over one hundred Whiting Brothers gas stations spanning the Southwest. Ultimately, grocery stores and motels were added to some locations. New Mexico alone had nine stations on Route 66, three of which were in Albuquerque. What made their businesses so profitable was their motto, "Gas For Less."

All that remains of many Whiting Brothers locations are the bright yellow and red signs.

To keep expenses down, they built their stations with concrete block and wood from their sawmill business in Arizona. They even hauled their own gas from the refineries. In addition, they painted bright yellow and red signs on wood instead of using neon. Some of these signs were like fences, 100 feet long, stretching into the desert landscape. Drivers could see these yellow signs in the distance and know that there was a Whiting Brothers station ahead. The attendants didn't wear fancy uniforms, and the gas prices were always a couple of cents cheaper than their competitors. They encouraged repeat customers by offering their own courtesy card. If you presented the card at another Whiting Brothers station, you were given an additional one cent per gallon discount.

During the Dustbowl of the 1930s, Midwest farmers, suffering years of devastating droughts and high winds, lost crops and livestock. Hundreds of people packed up what belongings they could fit in their jalopies, strapped a mattress on top, and headed to California for jobs in the land of fruit and honey. Whiting Brothers, aware of the travelers' meager cash, allowed these destitute migrants to repair their radiators or patch their worn tires using the station's tools. Usually there were barrels in the back filled with used oil given away for free. Naturally word got around and these desperate families would purchase all their gas at Whiting Brothers stations.

By the early 1970s America's road systems were changing. Route 66 was being circumvented by travelers preferring the faster east-west route of Interstate 40. The Whiting Brothers Corporation saw the writing on the wall and sold most of their properties.

Much of the information contained in this narrative was derived from the article, "Whiting Bros. Gas for Less," written by Johnnie Meier, which appeared in the *Route 66 New Mexico Magazine*, Spring 2019 issue, published by the New Mexico Route 66 Association.

Grants

Exits 85, 81 off I-40

"City of Spirit"

In 1880 the three Grant brothers—Angus, John, and Lewis— were contracted by the Atlantic and Pacific Railroad to lay tracks west of Albuquerque. To facilitate this undertaking, they set up a camp referred to as Camp Grants, then Grants Station until, in its final incarnation, simply Grants.

The arrival of the train spurred a new industry for the area—logging—with timber harvested from the nearby forested Zuni Mountains. The logs could be shipped quickly from Grants to a sawmill in Albuquerque and turned into lumber.

By 1939, however, the logging industry slumped and the area around Grants turned to farming. The rich volcanic soils were perfect for growing carrots. Grants became known as the "Carrot Capital of the United States." One can visit the Double 6 Gallery at the Route 66 Vintage Museum in Grants where enlarged postcards from this era are on display.

In 1950 Paddy Martinez of Navajo-Irish descent, being both a medicine man and prospector, was hired by the Anaconda Mining Company for $400 a month to scout for uranium in the area surrounding Grants. As the story goes—one day, tired of riding his horse, Paddy took a *siesta* in the shade of a tree. When he awoke he noticed a yellow rock close by, picked it up, and took it home. The analysis report came back—uranium ore! Paddy's discovery near Haystack Mesa turned Grants into a roaring mining town, a boom that lasted thirty years. In appreciation, a park in the center of town was named for Paddy.

After 1980 the demand for uranium collapsed, and the fortunes of Grants again declined. More recently, however, there's been an economic comeback with the growth of tourism. Visitors are drawn to the outdoor activities near Grants, to the beauty of the surrounding area, and, of course, a ride down Route 66 (Santa Fe Avenue) that runs through the middle of town.

Public art projects such as the *Native Basket Array* are positioned along Route 66, and a new mural project will be embellishing the outsides of buildings in town. On weekends and holidays, the local Fire and Ice Park is packed with townsfolk and tourists enjoying music, dancing, flea market shopping, holiday events, and indulging in the local cuisine from food trucks. Just across the street, cars and motorcycles line up to pass through the Route 66 Neon Drive-Thru for a photo op, enjoying the Mother Road in the "City of Spirit."

Milan

Exits 81 and 79 off I-40

Snakes and Snacks

Traveling west on Route 66 from Grants, you will take the bridge over the railroad tracks and arrive in the Village of Milan.

Fresh out of the military service, Herman Atkinson and his wife Phyllis headed to New Mexico in 1946 where his two older brothers, Leroy and Jake, had already established prospering trading posts along Route 66. Herman, too, wanted to take advantage of the ever-increasing tourist trade now that World War II rationing of gasoline and tires was over.

Herman soon opened Lost Canyon Trading Post just west of Grants. He stocked high-end Navajo rugs and jewelry, installed gas pumps, added a restaurant, followed by a "must stop" attraction—a three-legged bear. He fenced it in and taught the bear to drink sodas straight out of the bottle. Tourists would purchase a bottle of soda pop and hand it to the bear. This was an accident waiting to happen. And it did.

One day a woman offered the bear a soda, sticking the bottle through the fencing. The bear grabbed the soda and bit off one of her fingers. Turns out that finger was worth mega bucks. Her insurance company sure thought so.

Down the road, Herman's brother's trading post was advertising live rattlesnakes, and cars were pulling in by droves. Herman realized tourists were looking for cheaper souvenirs plus a Western thrill. So Herman's next inspiration was to bring in cobras which led to a name change for his business to Atkinson's Cobra Gardens. As customers increased, so did the exotic snake varieties: pythons, boa constrictors, rattlesnakes, and other species. Amazingly, 80,000 people paid ten cents each to view his reptile collection in 1949.

By 1950 there were 300 to 400 snakes slithering in a room-sized pit dug inside his trading post. Ringed with a protective railing, tourists could lean over the pit as Herman lectured and handled the squirming snakes below. The snake pit was also a source of amusement for local residents having few options for live entertainment. Local folks would congregate around the pit at feeding time and watch the snakes feast on a smorgasbord of mice, frogs, salamanders, and even bugs. On occasion onlookers might witness the boa constrictor swallowing a live chicken.

When a rumor began circulating that a highway bypass might be built, Herman decided early on to pull up stakes and head for Arizona before business fell off. Although he no longer wanted to be a snake handler, he still cared for the well-being of his reptilian captives. He once took a sick snake for an x-ray in a nearby doctor's office. The doctor wouldn't touch the snake but his wife volunteered to hold it still. When word spread that this largest collections of cobras in the United States was for sale, a multitude of buyers responded. The python alone sold for $300 and the rest of the collection was snapped right up.

The Thigpen family purchased Cobra Gardens around 1954. Having no interest in snakes, they renamed the tourist stop Cactus Gardens. Today only a small portion of the once long rambling structure still exists. A partial mural is visible out front but it is fast fading.

A few years ago I stopped by the location to check on the mural's condition and spoke to the new owner. She and her husband were in the process of remodeling the building for their business. She mentioned that during the renovation she was aghast to find snake skeletons.

Cowboy Coffee Sign, Milan, New Mexico

Part V
Narratives

From Milan to Beautiful Mountain Trading Post

Bluewater Outpost
Old Crater Trading Post
Rattle Snake Trading Post
Prewitt
Tomahawk Bar
Thoreau
Herman's Garage

Bluewater Outpost

Exit 72 off I-40

Curios Galore!

As you zip along I-40 that roughly parallels Route 66 west of Grants, you can't miss the string of billboards advertising the tourist treasures to be found at the Bluewater Outpost. Exit 72 brings you to this travel center nestled between the new highway and the old. It is one of several owned and operated by Bowlin Travel Center, Inc.

Here you will find the typical amenities: gasoline, clean restrooms, ice cream sundaes, hamburgers. It also offers tourists bolo ties with rattlesnake head clasps, a wild and wide selection of humorous T-shirts, serapes, moccasins, jewelry, and enough fireworks to ignite the sky for hours if not days. But it is the vast collection of hundreds of inexpensive knickknacks—from Native American themed refrigerator magnets to little green aliens and gaudy ceramic buffalo—that boggle the imagination. It's a curio collection on steroids.

The Bluewater Motel

Driving a few hundred yards north from the Outpost parking lot brings you to the intersection of old Route 66. Turn right. Continue about a mile east, and you will find the defunct Bluewater Motel set back from the road.

However, the old Bluewater Motel sign still stands near the road. Unlike many Route 66 neon signs that have been trashed or disappeared into the possession of collectors, this one remains on the site as of this writing. It is **not** for sale.

The owner and a few family members currently reside on the property. Last time I visited this location, the owner—an elderly gentleman—came out to speak with me. He said that the building next door had been a cafe and a bar, where folks came to eat, drink, and dance. He reminisced that it was "a lively place on a Saturday night."

Old Crater Trading Post

Exit 72 off I-40

Claude Bowlin, Friend of the Navajos

The year was 1912. The place was Gallup, New Mexico, where Claude Bowlin's career began as a merchandise trader dealing exclusively with the Navajos. In 1936 he left Gallup to open the original Old Crater Trading Post near Bluewater, New Mexico, alongside the dusty unpaved Route 66.

Once again he traded mostly with the Navajos, with his store carrying canned goods, horse tack, and some basic clothing—jeans, boots, and long-sleeved shirts for the Navajo men and velvet yardage for blouses and skirts for the women. He built corrals, vats for dipping and disinfecting sheep, and sheds for shearing them. There was always a pot of free coffee perking on the wood stove ready for his mostly Navajo customers.

As his business increased, Claude initiated community activities for the neighboring Navajos, buckboard races, and other competitive games. They came in droves to participate in these entertaining events and for a chance to socialize. Soon his trading post became the community center. The Bowlin family and the Navajos had high regard for each other. As an example of this mutual respect, a Navajo family asked Claude and his wife to raise one of their boys. That arrangement eventually led to the boy, Tom, being elected the first Navajo senator to the New Mexico State Legislature.

By 1938 Route 66 was completely paved and automobile traffic increased accordingly. Taking advantage of the new tourist trade, Bowlin added gas pumps and stocked a few handmade souvenirs. As demand increased for locally made crafts, Claude made room inside his building to install Navajo silversmiths and weavers. Customers could watch the creation of the traditional merchandise the store was selling. It was a clever marketing ploy because the Southwest was one of the few places people could actually see Native Americans and the picturesque landscape that was promoted in calendars and magazines circulating nationally.

After World War II when gasoline was no longer rationed, more people traveled the country's highways for recreation. Claude Bowlin and his family expanded their business by building additional stores in eastern and southern New Mexico.

The remains of the Old Crater Trading Post seen in the photograph is not the original building. This structure was built in 1954. It closed in 1973 after the construction of I-40, the preferred route for speedy travel. The loss of travelers along old Route 66 forced many trading posts to close. After Claude Bowlin died, his widow sold the property. As of 2006, the Old Crater Trading Post was listed on the National Registry of Historic Places.

Rattle Snake Trading Post

Exit 72 off I-40

Dining, Dancing, and Snakes

The attraction of live rattlesnakes at tourist stops along New Mexico's Route 66 was an oft repeated theme. Located between Bluewater and Prewitt on Route 66, the Rattle Snake Trading Post was first owned by Victor Holmes under the name Brock Trading Post. Holmes's initial attempt to lure passing travelers was to tie a couple of old burros next to the gas pumps. While tourists were busy taking photos, he was filling up their gas tanks. His second attraction was cock fights.

Jake Atkinson, a hunchback crippled by polio and scoliosis, never let his disabilities slow him down. Over the years, with his outgoing personality, he wound up running several successful trading posts in New Mexico. After Jake and his wife Maxine bought the Brock Trading Post in 1945, they quickly renamed it Rattle Snake Trading Post, kept the burros, and continued the cock fights that raged into the night. A donkey named Homebrew roamed the grounds, surreptitiously nibbling sandwiches and snacks out of overheated cars with doors and windows left open while the parched travelers sought shade and a cold soda in the store.

To attract more business, the Atkinsons displayed some of the biggest rattlesnakes ever found, purchased from a self-described Texas snake wrangler. This was such a hit, more snake pits featuring a variety of species were soon added.

More reptiles drew more tourists. Jake, ever wanting to expand business, came up with a new gimmick. Billboards were placed along Route 66 claiming "Next Stop See Giant Prehistoric Reptile 48 Feet Long." This turned out to be forty-eight feet of cow vertebrae stretched along the trading post's floor. A cow's pelvis was embedded into Plaster of Paris becoming the snake's head. Teeth and a horn were added, giving it a more fearsome appearance.

The Atkinsons ultimately added a cafe and a night club. Local folks flocked there on weekends, dancing to the tunes of The Dude Wranglers 'til the wee hours of the morning.

By 1951 the Atkinsons decided to sell the trading post to Maxine's sister and husband, Pauline and Carl Gibbs. As fate would have it, right after the sale, Rattle Snake Trading Post burned to the ground. Losing no time, Gibbs began rebuilding it.

Eventually Rattle Snake Trading Post, like many other tourist stops along Route 66, succumbed to the impact of I-40 bypassing the Mother Road. It closed for good in the '70s.

Prewitt

Exit 63 off I-40

More Trading Post Histories

Brothers Harold and Bob Prewitt opened the Prewitt Trading Post in 1917 in the community known as Baca, located west of Grants. After awhile the residents started calling the store Prewitt while the local Navajos referred to it as *Kin Ligaii* meaning "White House." The Prewitt Trading Post's main customers were the local Navajos who brought in rugs, wool, and jewelry in exchange for money to purchase the supplies they needed. Eventually, the brothers cooked up a scheme whereby they minted their own tokens to pay the Navajos for their wares instead of US dollars. The Indians were then forced to use these tokens which were only of value at the Prewitt store.

In 1946, to cash in on the Route 66 tourist trade, Justin and Odessa LaFont bought the Prewitt Trading Post, renaming it Justin's Trading Post.

A year later T. B. Greer arrived and built his trading post right next door to Justin's. Greer featured gas pumps, a cafe, and a motel. Greer named his establishment the "Zuni Mountain Trading Post." Just a year after opening, Greer sold his operation to Dave and Betty Ortega.

Up until the 1950s when uranium was discovered, the two trading posts competed for travelers' business. The nearby uranium operation drew many miners to town. The Ortegas decided to close the cafe and just serve the mining community plus the Indian trade. This left the tourist dollars to Justin's Trading Post.

Dave Ortega came from a family of traders owning stores in Arizona and New Mexico starting with his grandfather Thomas Ortega. When he bought the Zuni Mountain Trading Post he was well versed in trading rugs and jewelry. He ran a fair operation and was well liked by the Navajos. Before long he built a huge business selling Navajo jewelry throughout the country.

As was often the case throughout sparsely populated regions, the post office was located within the Zuni Mountain Trading Post, and Betty Ortega was the postmistress. After her husband Dave died in 1980, she leased the building several times to go-getters who immediately painted over the Zuni Mountain name and replaced it with their own. Throughout this period, the post office remained inside the building with Betty in charge. All along she was advocating for the construction of a new post office building. Even after a separate post office was finally built, she continued as postmistress, serving the community for twenty-five years.

When I visited Prewitt in 2020, the post office was the only lively place in town. As several Navajo old timers were leaving the premises, I asked them, "Whereabouts was the Ortega trading post?" They all immediately mentioned Betty and pointed to the abandoned building next door as the Zuni Mountain Trading Post.

Tomahawk Bar

Exit 63 off I-40

A Reinvented Quonset Hut

"Pistol Pete" South built the Tomahawk Bar in 1941 near Prewitt, New Mexico. To say it was a building might be an exaggeration as it probably came to life as just a small adobe brick structure. As such, it wasn't fated to endure.

Shortly after World War II it burned to the ground, and Pistol Pete began searching for a cheap and easy way to replace his watering hole. He struck pay dirt when he discovered that the United States government was offering its surplus pre-fabricated Quonset huts for sale. He placed an order for one in 1947 and was serving drinks shortly thereafter.

The Tomahawk Bar existed as a wet bar for decades. However, with a reputation for frequent fights, out-and-out brawls, and liquor law violations, it finally closed around 2010. Today it operates as a package liquor store and seems to be thriving. A steady stream of cars and pickups continue to belly up to the front door, park for several minutes as drivers dash in to make a purchase, and then drive away.

There is some random information under the heading "Some people say…." that the building once operated as a trading post specializing in castings and molds for silver jewelry. This tidbit certainly adds interest but I'm not sure about its authenticity.

About Quonset Huts

In 1941 Quonset Point, Rhode Island, lent its name to a unique, pre-fabricated structure that was inexpensive, strong, and easily assembled. It became a military staple throughout World War II to house everything from humans to field hospitals to offices—even latrines. Over 150,000 were manufactured during the War and offered for purchase to the public once the military began downsizing.

In fact, my parents considered purchasing land in California and using an inexpensive Quonset hut as our home—an idea which I find astounding that my mother would entertain. They ended up building an adobe house instead on the side of a hill in Morgan Hill. Thank goodness!

Thoreau
Exit 53 off I-40

From Rugs to Rubble

When first constructed in 1926, Route 66 meandered back and forth several times across the railroad tracks between Prewitt and Thoreau (pronounced "Threw").

From 1936 to 1937 parts of Route 66 were upgraded, and this stretch of eleven miles was one of them. The positive impact was that the straightened road now ran parallel to the railroad tracks, removing hazardous crossings for automobile traffic. The downside was that the Mother Road lay to the south of the tracks, and Thoreau sat on the north side. Travelers driving Route 66 no longer passed through town.

One day, while exploring Route 66, I decided to check out Thoreau. Driving around the side streets I was surprised to find a building that looked vaguely like an old curio shop. I could decipher faint lettering: NAVAJO RUGS and HANDMADE JEWELRY. What could it be doing here, surrounded by doublewides and modest homes on a dead end street? I took a photo anyway.

Several years later I returned to take another look. I drove slowly up and down all the graveled streets but couldn't find the building anywhere. Where did it go? I spotted a brand new mobile home near a pile of rubble and debris. The owner of the double-wide stepped out of his door to scrutinize me.

"Wasn't there a curio shop here?" I asked.

He nodded towards the debris pile. "You're looking at it."

I was shocked. Then he added, "Back in the '30s, that old building was originally on the old Route 66 before the road was straightened out. Then it was moved here but went out of business when I-40 came through. Not much to look at now."

As I snapped a photo of the remains, I sadly had to agree.

Herman's Garage
Exit 53 off I-40

Gas and Repairs

The building destined to become Herman's Garage began in Grants selling gas in 1935. Two years later it was moved thirty miles west to Thoreau, New Mexico, where, as a Standard Oil station, it offered gasoline plus a few car repairs. This is where Roy T. Herman was first employed after his military service.

Roy T. Herman was born in Texas in 1919. His family moved to Thoreau when he was still in elementary school. After finishing eighth grade, he attended the nearest high school in Fence Lake, 96 miles away. Until he graduated, Herman, like many kids from rural New Mexico, boarded in Fence Lake during the school months. There he met his high school sweetheart who became his wife.

In 1942, with the advent of World War II, Herman joined the military. He was assigned to the Army Air Corp where his first job was driving a fuel truck and gassing up aircraft before take-off. This sparked his interest in airplane mechanics and how to repair them. Soon Herman outpaced the other repairmen with his quick and accurate maintenance work.

When the war ended and he was discharged, Herman returned to Thoreau, securing his first civilian job at the Standard Oil station. He not only pumped gas but attended to the mechanical needs of cars and trucks traveling Route 66. In the early 1950s he was able to buy the station and moved the building 200 yards down the road. Focusing solely on vehicle repairs, he called it Herman's Garage.

Herman's Garage is no longer open for business. A collection of defunct trucks and cars surround the front as though waiting to be repaired. You can, however, drive up, park just off the pavement, and take a picture or two. Be advised: People live in the back and two dogs will come roaring out to keep you at a respectful distance.

Part VI
Narratives

From Beautiful Mountain Trading Post to the Arizona Border

Continental Divide
Tourist Stop
Gallup
Chief Yellowhorse

Continental Divide Tourist Stop

Elevation 7,263' (Officially)
Exit 47 off I-40

"Top o' the World" Tourist Stop

Homesteader Alma Gaines settled down on acreage at the Continental Divide around 1925. When Route 66 was graded past her property, she and her second husband decided to open two unrelated businesses—a gas station and a dance hall. As tourist trade increased, she sold some parcels of land to other wheeler-dealers who expanded a variety of traveler services and amusements.

One of the first buyers was a Texan named "Dee" Westbrook who opened a cafe and a bar. He quickly noticed that other trading posts featured animals so he began collecting some local wildlife. He started with Topey, a stuffed rattlesnake that was housed behind glass for "safety reasons", of course. Westbrook explained to kids that Topey was very mad but was sleeping now and they had "better be careful" not to wake him up because Topey was very dangerous.

Next, a couple of live bears joined the menagerie, followed by a mountain lion named Leo and Toughy the monkey. As the story goes, Toughy would sit on the bar all day smoking cigarettes and flicking the burning butts onto the seated customers. If a little girl arrived with her parents, Toughy would jump down from the bar, dash over to her, hike up her skirt, and spank her right on the bottom.

As the tale continues, one day Leo escaped his chicken-wire pen out back and ran around front near the entrance. Loudspeakers were blaring, cars started honking, people began hollering. Leo became so scared he ran toward the bar only to be greeted at the door by Toughy. One chomp and Toughy was no more. That left the screaming customers scrambling for safety. When the cook finally opened the kitchen door, Leo bolted through and made a beeline for his only known refuge—his pen.

A huckster, Lee Neal, showed up and built what appeared to be a comfortable, family-friendly hotel. However, in the back rooms there was some heavy-duty gambling going on. When a couple of his old carny friends arrived, they helped separate tourists from their dollars with shell games and card tricks. Their modus operandi was to let the unsuspecting visitors "win" a few rounds, at which point, the newcomers were encouraged to increase the amount of their bets. Inevitably, at game's end, the novices had been fleeced.

Over time, the businesses grew seedier and seedier. By 1960, brawls, a topless bar, and ladies of the night were the norm. The businesses provided a wild and unsavory rest stop not fit for the vacationing families motoring along Route 66.

Today this collection of stores has evolved from its disreputable Wild West days to a quiet tourist attraction

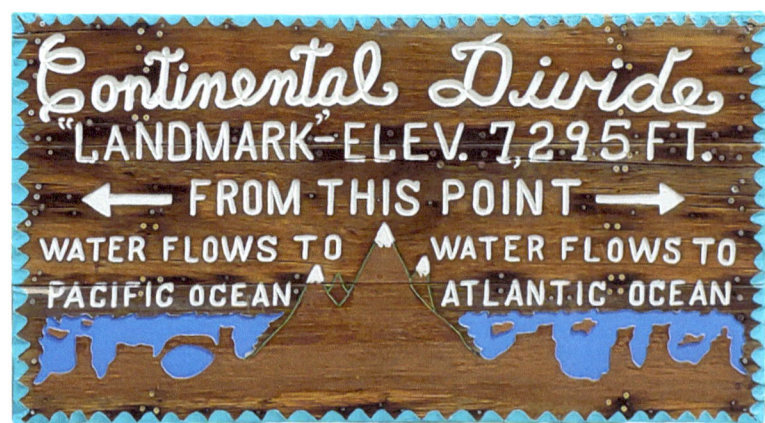

Sign outside the Continental Divide Tourist Stop declaring the elevation at this location.

with several curio shops featuring Route 66 souvenirs and memorabilia. The location also provides a photo op for people to plant a foot on the east and west sides of the Continental Divide—at the same time.

Some great stories about the history of Top O' the World and other Route 66 trading posts are written in Thomas Arthur Repp's book, *Route 66, the Romance of the West*.

Gallup
Exits 26, 22, 20, 16, 12 off I-40

The Heart of Red Rock Country

In order to extend tracks through the territories of western New Mexico and into Arizona, the Atlantic Pacific railroad company set up headquarters in the vicinity of what is now the city of Gallup. The year was 1880. Both New Mexico and Arizona were thirty-two years away from statehood.

At that time, David Gallup was the paymaster for the company. On Friday afternoons, when the workers were eager to collect their wages, they'd announce, "I'm going to Gallup." A year later, with the tracks completed, people began settling the growing city named Gallup.

In those days, as is today, a road paralleled the tracks where saloons and other businesses soon sprang up. When Route 66 came through Gallup in 1926, an ever-increasing stream of tourists began driving through town in need of services. Motels, gas stations, and restaurants were opened to accommodate them.

An added attraction were the many Indian trading posts that sold jewelry, rugs, and crafts made by the surrounding tribes. This created an industry that benefited both the Native Americans and Gallup businessmen as tourists flocked to the shops. Gallup quickly became known as the Southwest's center for high-quality, hand-crafted Native American wares. One of the original businesses that is still open today on Route 66 is Richardson's Trading Post which continues to deal in pawn and trade. I was told they had over one hundred saddles in the back that were brought in for trade.

Gallup, being the heart of Red Rock Country and Navajoland, hosts the annual Inter-Tribal Indian Ceremonial held at Red Rock Park. People travel from near and far to attend the festivities which include parades, rodeos, dances, music, arts and crafts vendors, traditional foods, plus many other contests and activities. This tribal gathering has been held annually for over ninety-eight years and remains an exciting and vibrant event.

El Rancho Hotel
Exit 22 off I-40

Where the Movie Stars Stayed

In the early 1930s, R. E. Griffith, brother of the legendary D. W. Griffith of silent movie fame, most likely was on a road trip along the newly opened Route 66. When he stopped in Gallup, he became inspired by the beauty of the vast landscapes and the richness of the surrounding Native American cultures. He realized this was ideal country for filming Western movies which were becoming a craze at the time. Seeing a business opportunity, he built a hotel along Route 66 in Gallup naming it El Rancho Hotel.

It soon became the headquarters for movie productions and a first-class, home-away-from-home for

Hollywood's movie stars. Mae West, Humphrey Bogart, Katherine Hepburn, Tom Mix, Rosalind Russell, Kirk Douglas, Doris Day, Gregory Peck, Lucille Ball, and Ronald Reagan were among the 158 actors who stayed there. In fact, all the hotel rooms were named after many of these actors—their names engraved on plaques above the doors.

The hotel, with its Western flavor, was also used as a stage set for scenes in the movies. The hotel lobby's rustic decor of dark, stained wooden balustrades and lodge pole beams, resembled a Western—yet elegant—hunting lodge. The two converging staircases to the second floor were covered in lush red carpeting.

It also housed a popular bar. During filming, it became the favorite hangout, earning Wild West fame for the drinking, gambling, brawling, and loud ragtime music. It has been reported that during raucous evenings, Errol Flynn would ride his horse into the hotel, right up to the bar, and order a drink.

By the early 1960s, public interest in Western films waned and the El Rancho fell into disrepair. At some point, Armand Ortega, a wealthy local trader, bought the hotel and restored it to its days of glory. He covered the walls with dozens of old photographs of movie stars who had lodged there during its heyday. In 1988 El Rancho Hotel was listed in the National Register of Historic Places.

Today it has a New Mexican restaurant and a great gift shop with authentic handcrafted jewelry made by the area's Native American tribes. The rooms are small by today's standards but the place is unique and well worth a stop, a bite, and a stay. And the movie stars' names above the doors still remain.

Over 80 famous Hollywood stars have stayed at El Rancho, noted by the brass plates on the rooms' doors.

Ortega's Indian Jewelry Heaven
Exit 20 off I-40

Looking for fine authentic Navajo, Zuni or Hopi jewelry? If it says Ortega's, you're in the right spot.

Armand Ortega, born in 1928, began his first years in Holbrook, Arizona, right near the Petrified Forest. Several years later his parents moved to Lupton, a small Arizona community on the Navajo Reservation just a stone's throw from the New Mexico border. There he saw tourists and Dust Bowl migrants passing by his front door on Route 66. He started his first business enterprise as a kid, standing out by the road selling petrified wood for a quarter to fifty cents apiece. Sometimes he collected $1.50 a day.

At age thirteen, Armand started working with his dad at a gas station for a couple of years. Thinking of his petrified wood venture, Armand convinced his dad Max to open their first store at the border selling jewelry and curios made by their Navajo neighbors. To make ends meet, Max took a job at the Inspection Station nearby, leaving their shop in Armand's hands. Saving his money over the years, Armand was able to purchase his first store west of Deming, New Mexico. This was the beginning of Ortega's booming Indian Market jewelry business across the Southwest.

In the 1980s Armand noticed the El Rancho Hotel was sliding into disrepair. At a bankruptcy auction in 1986, he purchased the hotel and spent two years restoring the rooms. It was ready for guests by 1988. Of course, a high-end jewelry shop was included near the lobby.

Armand Ortega passed away in 2014 but Ortega's Family Enterprises lives on. Their gift shops continue to expand across the country including national monuments and parks.

Chief Yellowhorse

Easy exit at #359 (Lupton, Arizona)
Turn right onto north Frontage Road; go 1/2 mile east

"Make Chief Great Again"

The Yellowhorse family has been in business for at least three generations, and like many other Route 66 roadside enterprises, moved with the Road.

The Yellowhorse family started selling Navajo rugs and petrified wood from a wooden stand beside Route 66 in the 1950s. They were friendly to the travelers who stopped by to inspect the blankets spread out on the table. They shared stories of reservation life that the tourists enjoyed, and their stand became a popular pull off.

By 1965, with business increasing, Juan Yellowhorse and his brother Frank moved their wares into the former Old Miller Trading Post on Route 66—right on the Arizona–New Mexico border—and changed the name to Fort Chief Yellowhorse. A wide, red line designating the state border was painted on the floor of the log *hogan* building. Tourists enjoyed straddling the line, placing one foot in New Mexico to the east and the other foot in Arizona on the west.

Set back from the Road and backed by a huge open cave in the red rock, the location was also known as "Chief Yellowhorse Hole in the Wall." Gas pumps were added, and many curios and Native American handmade items filled the shelves of the shop. David Yellowhorse recalls that when he was just a youngster, all the Yellowhorse kids were taught to greet the tourists with a friendly smile. They encouraged visitors to purchase more items than they had planned on. Following his family's entrepreneurial spirit, David rode his donkey around the place and offered twenty-five cent rides to children waiting for parents to gas up their cars or browse the souvenirs. The place also corralled live buffalo and goats for the tourists to see.

Nowadays, the business is called "Chief's Cave." The Fort is still standing along with the yellow dinosaur yard sculpture, and a few horses roam freely around the property. The easiest way to arrive at this location is to take exit #359 off I-40 (Lupton, Arizona), turn right onto the north frontage road (Old Route 66), and drive a half mile east. Chief's Cave will be on the north side of the road. You can't miss it. Just look for the sign "MAKE CHIEF GREAT AGAIN."

With traffic flying by on I-40, the family opened a second location named Chief Yellowhorse Trading Post in Arizona, just over the New Mexico state line, right at Exit 359 off I-40. Large red and yellow signs advertise the locale; and animal sculptures were placed on the rock ledge above the shop long ago to catch the eye of travelers. Over the years, this location expanded into a complex of multiple buildings along the north frontage road, owned and operated by various family members offering authentic Native American made items.

The Chief Yellowhorse business is one of the oldest Navajo owned enterprises on the Navajo Reservation. With a backdrop of high, spectacular sandstone painted cliffs, this area is one of the most scenic locations found along Route 66.

Juan Yellowhorse passed away in 1999; brother Frank died in 2022. However, the Yellowhorse offspring continue to produce fine Native American crafts sold around the world.

The Arizona-New Mexico state line runs right through the center of the original Chief Yellowhorse Trading Post.

Contributing Authors

The following writers generously contributed selected narratives to this book:

Dorothy E. Noe
Freelance writer for *The Sandoval Signpost*, Placitas, New Mexico, *New Mexico Magazine*, Santa Fe, New Mexico, and other publications.

Don Bullis
New Mexico Centennial Author. Author of *New Mexico Historical Chronology 2018*, *Bloodville*, *No Manure on Main Street*, *Old West Trivia Book*, and others.

Johnnie Meier
Project Manager for New Mexico Route 66 Corridor Neon Restoration, Past President of New Mexico Route 66 Association, owner of Classical Gas Museum in Embudo, New Mexico, and a Route 66 preservationist.

Joan Fenicle
Artist and author, Placitas, New Mexico.

Sources

When my interest in Route 66 was first sparked in 2012, I unwittingly began this book solely as a photographer, packing my cameras, my lunch, and my dog into my 4Runner for a day trip or weekend exploration of The Mother Road from my home base in Albuquerque. Trained as a fine arts painter at the University of California, Davis, I was drawn to photograph what was visually exciting, beautiful, colorful, emotive, or curious to me. Over several years, my inventory of photographs taken along Route 66 grew to quite a collection.

Along the way I met folks who had lived all, most, or a good part of their lives in the same New Mexico town or village. They willingly shared their memories, recollections, and memorabilia about Route 66 from "back in the day." These stories and nuggets of information peaked my curiosity to research and identify what I had captured with my camera. I turned to libraries, historical associations, books, magazines, and the internet as noted below to assist me in my search.

Online Sources

- A Website of Road Travel America, www.route66roadtrip.com
- El Rancho Hotel, elranchohotel.com
- El Rey Court, elreycourt.com
- Ghost Towns USA and Canada website, www.ghosttowns.com
- Historic Route 66 in New Mexico, www.route66guide.com
- Kansas Historical Society, www.kshs.org/kansapedia
- LaFonda on the Plaza, lafondasantafe.com
- Legends of America, www.legendsofamerica.com
- MrZip66 ("Story of the Longhorn Ranch on New Mexico Route 66"), mrzip66.com

- National Park Service, www.nps.gov
- National Register of Historic Places, www.nps.gov/subjects/nationalregister
- National Trust for Historic Preservation, www.savingplaces.org/places/historic-route-66
- Never Quite Lost, www.neverquitelost.com
- New Mexico True, www.newmexico.org
- Parametrix ("Route 66 & Native Americans"), www.parametrix.com
- RETRO 66 Relive the Route Committee, www.facebook.com/Relivetheroute
- Roadside New Mexico, www.roadsidenewmexico.com
- Route 66x10, www.Rt66.x10host.com
- Route 66 MC, www.route66mc.com
- Route 66 News, www.route66news.com
- Route 66 Times, www.route66times.com
- The City of Grants ("Welcome to the City of Grants: History"), www.cityofgrants.net/about-grants-nm
- *The Route 66* (blog), TheRoute-66.com
- Tucumcari and Quay County Then and Now, www.facebook.com/TucumcariNM
- Wikipedia, en.wikipedia.org
- Yellowhorse LTD, Navajoland, USA, www.yellowhorseLTD.com
- The Historical Committee Presents: "Hannett's Joke: Route 66" by Eric Scott Jeffries, State Bar of New Mexico, Spring 2000, pages 36-38, www.sbnm.org
- "From Bootlegging to Respectable, Silva's Saloon, Bernalillo, New Mexico," by Lanier, C. and Derek Hembree The Blog (2013, October 2, Updated 2017, December 6), HuffingtonPost.com
- Clip Art: NM Outline.png, Pixbay.com, CCO public domain

Magazines

- "Whiting Bros. Gas for Less," written by Johnnie Meier, which appeared in the *Route 66 New Mexico Magazine*, Spring 2019 issue, published by the New Mexico Route 66 Association.
- *The Sandoval Signpost*, Placitas, New Mexico

Books

- Monika Ghattas, *Los Arabes of New Mexico: Compadres from a Distant Land* (Sunstone Press, 2012)
- Paul Milan, "The Last Tourist Attraction" (Cibola County Historical Society)
- Thomas Arthur Repp, *Route 66: The Romance of the West* (Mock Turtle Press, 2002)
- Jack D. Rittenhouse, *A Guide Book to Highway 66* (University of New Mexico Press, 1989)
- Joe Sonderman, *Images of America: Route 66 in New Mexico* (Arcadia Publishing, 2010)

Note: The original paintings on the walls of Stone's Buffalo Trading Post, Santo Domingo Trading Post, and Old Crater Trading Post have been attributed to R. G. Ward, artist and creator of the Tinkertown Museum in Sandia Park, New Mexico, by his widow Carla Ward, author of *The Tinker of Tinkertown: The Life and Art of Ross Ward*.

If Not for Them ...

My greatest thanks goes to these four. I'm forever grateful. They have given me courage, support, and hours of their time. Without their belief in me and this book, it would still be a dream, swishing through my head, like always wanting to be a cowgirl.

Donna Van Diepen, my sister
Donna has been my stalwart supporter of all my endeavors, especially this one. At a moment's notice, she'd jump in the car and accompany me to check out a curio site or a neon sign, all the while taking copious notes for the book.

Carol L. Adamec, my friend
Carol scrutinized my every photograph, picked through all the narratives, and with all her artistic and business expertise, helped me select the most relevant. She gave me months of her time. Without her dogged persistence, parts of this book would be scattered around my desktop.

Dorothy Noe, my narrative editor
Dottie started me on this journey. One day she loaned me a book of photographs taken along the entire Route 66 from Chicago to Santa Monica. I thought, Geez, with all my photographs of Route 66, I could compile a publication of just New Mexico images. Dottie offered to edit my narratives. As I completed each one, she would have it edited within a couple of hours. I scrambled to keep up. She also research and composed several narratives included in this book for which I am grateful.

Alan Kennish, my friend and former partner
I went to art school and became a painter but enjoyed photography mostly during my travels to foreign countries. At the time I still used a film camera and had my photos printed at the local Walmart. However, it was Alan, a photographer himself who ran a digital printing business, who introduced me to the medium of fine art digital prints. It opened up an entire new world of fine art photography that I have pursued for the past twenty years. Alan's support and encouragement have been instrumental in my journey to create this book. From the get-go he cheered me on, saying it was "a fabulous idea."

...And Others

My heartfelt thanks goes to the many folks named here who provided their interest, encouragement, personal stories and histories that supported me in the creation and completion of this book: Betsy Barnett, Lynne Bonino, Ed Boles, Don Bullis, David and Clerice Carrillo, Gloria Carrillo, Carol Chamberland, Lenore Dillon, Linda Dillon, Adam Doody, Paul Evans, Joan Fenicle, Heather and Brad Ficklin, Kathy Flynn, Robert Gallegos, Ginger Golden, Ron Gole, Keith Gottlieb, Kevin Gottlieb, Nancy Harbert, Susan Harper, Pat Harris, Clarice Hedges, Andy House, Joanne Kamiya, Kit Keith, Orlando Lucero, Bob Mahon, Nan Masland, Janet McVicker, Johnnie Meier, Wendy Melvin, Paul Milan, Larry and Leda Mooreland, Fred Morton, Sheryl and Bill Neely, Christina Noftsker, Betty Jo Otten, Louise Pryor, Augustine Romero, Denise Silva, Gale Sutton, Darryl Thomas, Nancy Tucker, Barbara Van Cleve, Carla Ward, Robin Webb, Dan White, Scott Yellowhorse.

Final Words

When I was growing up, I was not aware that our family car trips from California to Arizona were on Route 66. I was more interested in the curio shops and tourist attractions that my parents insisted we avoid.

In college I traveled through the Southwest with friends, deciding in 1974 to move to New Mexico. I frequently drove back and forth to California to see my parents. By then, I-40 had replaced most of Route 66, except for a few segments here and there in sparsely populated areas. Still, I had little awareness of Route 66, its history and importance as America's first federal highway.

It was August 2012 when an old abandoned building off of I-40 near Bluewater, New Mexico, captured my attention. It had colorful paintings on the outside walls. A few days later I returned to the location with my camera to photograph the fading paintings and peeling signs covering the building. After a little research I found the site to be Bowlin's Old Crater Trading Post on Route 66.

That discovery sparked my passion to seek out Route 66 and piece together its history and stories in pictures. Where was the Route? What were these places with murals? Why are some places ghost towns and others are still thriving tourist attractions?

At home with my laptop, I researched old maps of Route 66 for access to locations and clues for finding sites from that bygone era. Exiting off the interstate, I followed old pavement and gravel roads. I got good at spotting concrete pads that once anchored gas pumps, faint lettering painted on buildings, vintage cafes and motels, hand painted cowboy and Indian murals, and the architectural styles of the era.

Often I returned to sites I had previously photographed. I was dismayed that a neon sign had disappeared, a wall or roof had collapsed, or a pile of cement and debris was what remained of a structure from the heydays of the Mother Road.

I joined the Route 66 Association of New Mexico and was glad to learn that government support, national and local groups, and individual enthusiasts were working to preserve and restore the vestiges of curio shops, trading posts, and way stations of Route 66.

In 1999 Congress established the Route 66 Corridor Preservation Program, providing funding to the National Park Service to identify, prioritize, and provide financial support for Route 66 preservation. Local groups and individuals in New Mexico have spent long hours working on preservation projects. Johnnie Meier of the New Mexico Route 66 Association was recently awarded a grant to create a video on neon sign repair. Longtime Albuquerque business owners Carlos and Ed Garcia have been rescuing New Mexico's neon signs before collectors take them out of state. The Garcias are in the process of restoring these neon signs with plans to have them on display once again.

The leaders of some New Mexico towns have rallied their businesses and residents to the cause of preservation and its benefits. Officials in Tucumcari made restoration of Route 66 a priority. Connie Loveland, Main Street Director, and Christy Dominguez, owner of Odeon Theatre, have focused on saving signs and buildings. Ruth Ann Litchfield, Mayor of Tucumcari, was instrumental in the passage of a neon sign ordinance to prevent the removal of vintage neon signs. La Cita Restaurant once again has its revolving sombrero sign working, delighting Tucumcari's locals and tourists driving the Mother Road through town. Grants, New Mexico, is attracting Route 66 enthusiasts with public art projects and a drive-thru 66 archway that provides a must-take photo op.

Thanks to collaborations between government agencies and organizations devoted to historical preservation, along with the efforts of private individuals, there are great examples of successfully restored sites in New Mexico. Among them are the reconstruction of the Santo Domingo Trading Post, the refurbished Midway Trading Post exterior near Edgewood, Stone's Buffalo Trading Post, *aka* Rosa's Cantina in Algodones, and restoration of the KiMo Theatre and El Vado Motel in Albuquerque to name a few. There is still much to be done.

So, is preserving Route 66 worthwhile? The National Trust of Historic Preservation established in 1949 was founded on that belief. Based in Washington, D. C., the organization focuses on advocacy, legislation, and fundraising to preserve and protect historic sites in America. A study done less than ten years ago by the National Trust reported that tourists traveling Route 66 spend more than $130 million each year.

And it's not just Americans doing the trip. During my ten years of exploring and photographing Route 66 here in New Mexico, I've met visitors from Norway, Luxembourg, and South Korea. One couple celebrated each of their children's 16th birthday with a family trip on Route 66. I talked to a young man from South Korea who was bicycling across America via Route 66. Why did these people come here? For the wide open spaces of New Mexico and the romance of our Western heritage. Being from countries without such grand vistas and unique natural beauty, they find this experience fulfills a need in their souls.

I hope that my photographs will inspire others to help preserve Route 66 and its iconic significance in American history.

–Sondra Diepen, 2022

About the Author

I always wanted to be a cowgirl.

I was lucky to be born to the right parents who loved horses and always had horses. In fact, they first met on horseback on a cattle drive and participated in horsemanship events during their marriage. The family album is full of pictures of them riding together out in wide open spaces.

We lived in California, out in the country, on ten acres near Morgan Hill before it was considered wine country. At age six, I started out with a pony. We had three horses: my "Tony the Pony", Bedouin (half Arabian, half Morgan), and a workhorse named Babe.

When I was ten my dad found me riding Bedouin bareback. He was a bit anxious since Bedouin had not been ridden in quite some time. On weekends I would ride four miles into town on horseback to see my friends because they were all "horse-crazy."

For my twelfth birthday my dad took me to San Francisco to have a beautiful, custom saddle made for me. I still have that saddle. And my folks took my sister Donna and me to a working cattle ranch in the Sierras where we rode horses twice a day, hiked mountain trails, and learned to love wide open spaces, too.

My parents also loved the Southwest, and we spent our family summer vacations in Arizona and New Mexico. Riding, hiking, and camping were all part of my childhood experiences and things I continued to enjoy in my college days and adult years.

I studied fine art and painting at the University of California, Davis, moved to New Mexico, taught elementary school, and traveled during summers to countries in the Middle East, Asia, and Central America. Instead of buying postcards, I took hundreds of slides on my travels. Back home, I would share my adventures and images with friends. I had a T-shirt business, printing my own designs and, after retiring from teaching, continued to paint.

I bought my first digital camera in 2008. When I saw the large, beautiful prints possible with this new technology, I gave up painting and turned to photography. Now, two Nikon digital cameras go everywhere with me.

A great day for me is packing a lunch, grabbing my cameras and a few maps, and taking off with my dog Zephyr. I wander around to see what catches my eye and take a picture of it. I never know what I'll discover around the next bend.

Sondra lives in rural Albuquerque with her dog, cat, and four chickens and enjoys a beautiful view of the Sandia Mountains from her patio.

Follow author/photographer Sondra Diepen online at Route66inNewMexico.com

www.ingramcontent.com/pod-product-compliance
Lightning Source LLC
Chambersburg PA
CBHW041116300426
44111CB00003B/68